THE SEAMLESS ENTERPRISE

Books authored or coauthored by Dan Dimancescu:

Global Stakes: The Future of High Technology in America, with Ray Stata and James Botkin, Ballinger, 1982

Deferred Future: World and Corporate Debt and Bankruptcy, Ballinger, 1983

The Innovators; Rediscovering America's Creative Energy, with Ray Stata and James Botkin, Harper & Row, 1984

The New Alliance: America's New R&D Consortia, with James Botkin, Ballinger, 1986

THE SEAMLESS ENTERPRISE

Making Cross Functional

Management Work

Lessons for executives and managers on
concurrent engineering, continuous improvement
and customer driven product development

DAN DIMANCESCU

 HarperBusiness
A Division of HarperCollins*Publishers*

HarperCollins books may be purchased for educational, business, or sales promotional use. For information, please call or write: Special Markets Department, HarperCollins Publishers, Inc., 10 East 53rd Street, New York, NY 10022. Telephone: (212) 207-7528; Fax: (212) 207-7222.

FIRST EDITION

Designed by Joan Greenfield

Library of Congress Cataloging-in-Publication Data

Dimancescu, Dan.
    The seamless enterprise : making cross functional management work / by Dan Dimancescu.
        p.   cm.
    "Lessons for executives and managers on concurrent engineering, continuous improvement, and customer driven product development."
    Includes index.
    ISBN 0-88730-544-X
    1. Organizational effectiveness.   2. Industrial management.
    I. Title.
    HD58.9.D56   1991   91-41605
    658–dc20   CIP

92 93 94 95 96 PS/HC 10 9 8 7 6 5 4 3 2 1

To Lewis Veraldi, 1930–1990,
whose vision inspired this book...

CONTENTS

CONTENTS

ACKNOWLEDGMENTS

Many people play vital and complementary roles in helping to bring a book to life. Books require a team effort, this one no less than others.

Over the years self-financed visits to Japan helped me through my own one-man training program in cross-function management. This would not have been possible without the open and generous time of many people devoted to answering my questions and introducing me to experts. I am particularly indebted to Dr. Toshiaki Fujimori of Shimizu Corporation, who participated in Dartmouth conferences on cross-function management and through whom I was introduced to Total Quality Management experts at the Japan Union of Scientists and Engineers (JUSE), key managers at other corporations, and management experts in academe. Among the latter I am particularly grateful to Professors Yoji Akao (Tamagawa University), Tadashi Yoshizawa (Tsukuba University) and assistant professor Hisakazu Shindo (Yamanashi University) for shepherding me through the subject.

ACKNOWLEDGMENTS

Through these individuals I met Takami Kihara, a young employee of Japan's largest software-development company, CSK. At their suggestion, I helped him to enter a master in engineering program at Dartmouth's Thayer School of Engineering. Takami and his new wife, Eriko, arrived in Hanover for a three-year stay. Takami, while he had a lot to learn about engineering practices, offered Dartmouth its first real insights into new TQM practices, particularly Quality Function Deployment techniques applied to software engineering.

Thanks, too, to Dean Charles Hutchinson of the Thayer School of Engineering for allowing me to chair several pioneering conferences on cross-functional management starting in 1988. These attracted the participation or support of innovative executives including Lewis Veraldi of Ford Motor Company, Jim Watson of Texas Instruments, and John Black of Boeing Commercial.

Numerous companies have opened their doors to me with little asked in return. Most notable to me are the insights garnered from Komatsu Tractor Division starting in 1984. Although I did not know it then, it was one of two companies that pioneered cross-function management in the 1960s. Other companies include Analog Devices/Japan (instruments and semiconductors), CSK (software), Fuji-Xerox (copiers), Japan Systems Corporation (software), Juki Industries (sewing machines), Kobayashi Kosei (cosmetics), NEC (computers and semiconductors), Sharp (electronics), Texas Instruments/Japan (semiconductors), Toshiba (laptops), and Yokogawa Electric (Hewlett Packard's partner company). I was always struck by the effort each company took to answer questions and to allow busy individuals the time to meet with me.

In the U.S., I am especially thankful to Ray Stata, founder and President of Analog Devices, Inc., with whom I co-authored two books on technology-related issues. His support and keen insights led to my first serious studies of Japan's industrial success story. I am also grateful to Digital Equipment Corporation for supporting the translation of Japanese management materials, including the book Cross-Function Management, by Kenji Kurogane, published by the Japan Standards Association.

AT&T, Boeing, Digital, and Hewlett-Packard, as client companies with which I consult, and the International Association for Electronic Product Development (IAEPD), a 15-company consortium I codirect, have all been valued supporters of research that would introduce them to methods and techniques encompassed under the heading of cross-function management. And my grateful appreciation to Bob Johansen and his colleagues at the Institute for the Future in Menlo Park, California, for understanding the potential of the cross-function model and the CFM/pro™ software my partner, Ron Cordes, developed to support cross-function teaming methods. Ron's effort was inspired by his own frustration with the limitations of the traditional project-management software that he had spent a major part of his career developing.

This publication project started with Carol Franco, my publisher on prior books and now with the Harvard Business Press, who suggested I meet Mike Snell. "He's the perfect book agent," she said. She was right. Mike got the ball rolling with enthusiasm and confidence. The discipline he imposed on my initial proposal forced coherence and structure on so broad a subject.

I am greatly obliged to Jim Childs and his successor Jennifer Hull, my editors at HarperBusiness, for risking a new subject on an audience of managers bombarded by all varieties of "how to" books. It was only when I started footnoting references that Harper's long and successful history with business titles struck me. It includes two famed figures: Frederick Winslow Taylor, whose collected works were printed by Harper & Brothers in 1947; and Peter F. Drucker, whose *Practice of Management* appeared a few years later, both of whom are referred to in this work. My own books have all been published by Harper or its subsidiaries. Roberta Tovey, a talented freelance editor, patiently reorganized the flow, edited phraseology, and offered invaluable insights. Absent her efforts, there would not have been a publishable book.

Reading early versions of a manuscript in progress was a volunteer effort by a variety of individuals. Al Viswanathan at Boeing Commercial's Quality Center, himself an avid student of quality management practices, was most generous in making suggestions and in trusting that something intelligible would result. So was Luigi D'Angola, whom I first knew when he was employed by Digital Equipment Corporation and later with his own consulting firm, Strategus.

ACKNOWLEDGMENTS

The day I submitted my manuscript to the publisher, I received a phone call from my brother, Dimitri. He had been editing the autobiography of my father, who died in 1985 at age 88. "You'll be interested in some details I found," he told me. Writing about his post–World War I military service as a foreign student from Romania at the Carnegie Institute of Technology (now called Carnegie-Mellon University), my father wrote: "In 1922 I received my degree with the title of engineer with highest marks in my class. Engineering has many branches and mine was quite new. Actually I was among the first Taylorist engineers at Carnegie Tech." He added, "we Taylorists were educated to measure and organize logically. We were called efficiency experts, later industrial engineers, and then management engineers." Although he went on to a career as a Romanian diplomat, those engineering skills helped him survive the loss of country and wealth when the Communist regime took over in 1947. Surprisingly, what my father saw as the "new" style in 1922 is still deeply entrenched in American business habits. Seventy years later, many people are finally aware of the obsolescence of the breakthroughs engineered by Frederick Winslow Taylor. This book is about a "new" post-Tayloristic management style helping to re-engineer American enterprise.

And if further thanks are due, there is my friendly Macintosh Portable. Even at 15 pounds it traveled easily to Asia, Europe, and across the country helping me write this book. Its makers will be happy to know that it has enough battery power to provide full service across the Pacific. The Mac brought pleasure, too, to my children, Katie and Nicholas, who may not have enjoyed the time I spent writing, but definitely enjoyed their turns with the mouse.

Thanks also to Katherine, my wife, who sustained the family's spirits and enthusiasm. Many times she provided me with pointed suggestions on how and where to improve the book—and also endured two house moves during all of it.

D.D.

FOREWORD

When I first traveled to Japan in 1966, the streets were still crowded with three-wheel chain-driven trucks, wooden clogs were as popular as Western shoes, and the dollar was worth 360 yen. But it was clear that Japan was racing forward to a new economic future. The country had already established "world class" brand names, as my professional photographer colleagues with their Nikon equipment could then well attest.

There was a lot then even in traditional culture to tell us how Western habits were studied and adapted. One of them seemed particularly fitting. Early Dutch travelers to the islands had found it difficult to eat the normal diet. To make some of the raw foods more palatable, they started to deep-fry them in a dusting of flour. Several hundred years later this habit had been translated into an undisputably Japanese national dish: *tempura*, or deep-fried foods in a light batter. Koreans, whose culture predates the Japanese, like to tell similar stories. The Japanese tea ceremony bowl, so subtly shaped to the touch of a hand, came from a Korean design.

FOREWORD

Twenty years after that first visit, my interest was on very different issues: management practices, for one. But a study of Japanese management told a story akin to the origins of tempura and tea bowls.

Back in the 1950s and 1960s, Japanese managers and academics saw opportunities in methods and techniques that were underappreciated in the United States. Contemporary Japanese management is in fact largely the best of American management innovations—gone west and right over the Pacific Ocean. W. Edwards Deming, guru of statistical process control, was an unrecognized name in the mainstream of American management until the 1980s. My 1977 edition of Peter F. Drucker's famed *Management: Tasks-Responsibilities-Practices* does not even reference Deming in the index. And the word *quality* does not have a single entry in the same 800-page volume! Even Harvard professor Michael Porter's early bestselling strategy books overlooked quality as a cornerstone to formulating truly world-class competitive strategies.

Americans need to revisit the origins of today's best-in-class management methods in order to relearn the business of producing customer-desired goods and services. Some set out to do this and to repatriate these ideas from Japan. I started in 1984, at a Komatsu tractor factory in Mooka City. I was accompanying a Japanese professor cum quality consultant and an MIT professor with whom I was considering writing a book on Deming's principles. This visit provided my first naive insights into quality management of which I knew very little. It would take more than seven years for those first impressions to finally crystallize into a book.

At Komatsu, I soon discovered that a joint venture with International Harvester was largely derided in not-too-subtle comments such as: "Well, IH machine is not so reliable."

During the visit, the plant manager, Mukai Hideo, invited us to observe several working meetings with members of his factory staff and the quality consultant. A translator whispered the interchanges to us in English simultaneously. The discussion focused on preproduction design of a new engine model and the test process needed to keep defects from occurring on the production line. One of them was a transmission problem. When a farmer shifted his tractor into reverse, a severe jolt would result.

Because farmers were often accompanied by their wives, the jolt had the double whammy of throwing both husband and wife to the ground. This was clearly a defect worth solving immediately.

The consultant pressed the 25 people present. "How good were your design standards if they allowed problems to occur later? Good information was not passed on."

One manager said, awkwardly, "during preproduction trials we were not able to check process capabilities because there were not enough actual engine units on which to do accurate tests."

"Can't you make more sample units earlier on?" queried the consultant, in a sharp and almost rude tone that would have been out of order in the United States. The give-and-take was relentless, searching for simple facts of omission and possible areas of improvement. What impressed me most was not just the palpable energy invested in improving quality, but that the whole development team was present in the room. This was a dedicated, cohesive team. It was learning to identify and solve problems together, not by pushing blame on any one person.

Near the end of the day, the plant manager shared a single 8×10-inch piece of paper with me. "The whole quality process is described here," he said. Team members, concurrent tasks and meetings, checkpoints, decisions, and standards that would collectively get them to "do things right" were all described with graphic flowchart symbols and a few words. An 8×10-inch single sheet described the whole process. I had seen nothing this elegant in its simplicity before. It struck me then as a masterful management tool. From it, all team members knew exactly what to anticipate, both for themselves and for their relationships with other team players.

To me, this single sheet represented a clue to a larger holistic concept of management. I was witnessing a team of people focusing on process with as much vigor as on results. I came to view this as a breakthrough in management style. In our world results were the primary focus, at any cost.

It took almost eight years of peripatetic visits to Japan, a lot of gathering of pieces, to finally give meaning to that single 8×10-inch sheet of paper. It became the basis for an innovative process-mapping technique that is described in detail in this book as "Four-Fields Mapping." I have come to recognize, also, that this same technique, still unbeknownst to its Japanese originators and contemporary users, can have a potentially far-reaching impact as a user-friendly interface for teams to electronically access data and documentation across networks.

During these first visits, watching the Japanese quality consultant at work was a hands-on lesson in the human side of process management. We traveled together to Komatsu, Texas Instruments' Semiconductor Plant in Kyushu, Toyo Rubber, Nissan, Yokogawa Electric, and other less-known companies. In each of these visits, senior managers and workers sat side-by-side enduring embarrassingly pointed questions about seemingly minor day-to-day problems. Taiyo Kogyo was an example. A rental company for displays, tents, and other group events equipment, it was tackling two serious quality problems. In 1975 an air-pressured tent had collapsed at a fair, causing the whole event to be closed for 40 days. Taiyo Kogyo lost face in a headlining news report. "Up to that time," said its founder and president, Hiromasa Nohmura, "we thought that just selling was enough. And top management thought it was quite a special skill to sell a defective product." Soon after the collapse incident, he introduced a total quality program. "It was not easy. The people around me did not believe it."

Ten years later, when I happened to visit, repairs of leaky seams were the subject of a session I attended at the Tokyo offices. The purpose was to resolve repeated complaints about leaking tents, a problem of particular severity in a country as rainy as Japan. In front of his employees, sitting at a U-shaped table, a manager was being pressed on the subject of leaky seams by the consultant. The conversation focused on deliveries from the warehouse.

CONSULTANT: "How did you determine the customer's standard of quality?"

MANAGER: "By shipping only those without defects."

CONSULTANT: "You mean those *you* think are good?"

MANAGER: "I consulted with salespeople."

CONSULTANT: "Are you confident salespeople can represent customers' needs? By what criteria?"

FOREWORD

MANAGER: "We depend on common sense. We eliminate items that a customer would reject as inferior."

CONSULTANT: "You did not base your decision on customer opinions? Who approved this?"
The nerves in his neck bulging, the manager's face turned red. He was being grilled right in front of his employees.

MANAGER: "It is not approved yet. We have only come up with photographs showing standards on what to ship and what not to ship."

CONSULTANT: "You are not checking your facts enough," interjected the consultant gruffly. "You are not being a manager enough. Come up with countermeasures *before* the problem occurs. Right now you are basing your judgment on imaginary needs. Get up-to-date data."

It took a while for me to digest the lessons of that meeting. One aspect stood out: not only were all the departments present around the table working as a single team, but they were being tutored in *cross-function* process management. The issue at hand and the communication between team members cut right across departmental boundaries. Customer service was the subject, not who had what responsiblity in any particular departmental chimney. These people were not only learning to improve their performance as a group, but also to *internalize* this knowledge across the whole team. Such group learning, painful and oftentimes slow, was something I witnessed time and again during this and other visits to Japan. The American way would have been to hire an expert to recommend a quick fix, or to have a departmental specialist dictate a solution. On either case the team does not internalize the problem or the solution; it only executes instructions without understanding. It has no sense of the total picture.

Our management style is a reflection of a long history of specialization, of scientific empirical analysis that separates the part from the whole. It goes back to the Cartesian divorce of mind from body, and three subsequent centuries of scientific theories and practices founded on these principles.

Contemporary management is a cultural reflection of these deeply held habits, biases, and reflexes built over decades and some cases centuries. At the end of the nineteenth century, Taylorism manifested the same Cartesian bias. Work, in Frederick Winslow Taylor's view, was a measurable commodity that could be broken into quantifiable parts and subjected to scientific analysis and control. Sequential task management evolved from this approach. One specialist hands off his specialized task to the next. The legacy of scientific management lives on today. But it no longer works. Its flaws are in losing sight of the totality of enterprise activity and in downplaying the subjective, or human side, as a key to successful management. Accelerating the need for a new holistic vision of management are other world forces. The most important is most easily understood through headline news articles about the fragility of the environment. This has made a large audience consider the complexity of "environmental ecosystems." A toxic dump is now treated much less as a final disposal solution than as a component of a wider ecological system. The burning of Amazonian forests or the Chernobyl disaster is now understood to have unexpected secondary effects far from its point of origin.

In the same fashion, the organizational fragmentation induced by scientific management is being replaced by holistic principles of management. We no longer find it acceptable that a company be treated as a collection of separate parts, each independent of the other. This realization is manifest in varied business initiatives. "Time-to-Market" is one of them. Getting products conceived and developed fast can only happen if companies work as teams, oblivious to artificial organizational walls. "Concurrent engineering" is another. To the Department of Defense, which is pushing its suppliers to function more effectively, concurrent engineering is a holistic product-development process bridging from concept to actual disposal. It represents a dramatically broader understanding of a product as part of a much wider set of issues and concerns.

Such realizations are not unique to business alone. America has set to work in the 1990s re-engineering its schools, its cities,

FOREWORD

its environment, and finally its management philosophy. The new paradigm treats parts as components of larger systems. This paradigm is what differentiates the management style discussed in this book from the Tayloristic ones grown obsolete.

The management style treated in this book views the company and its ways of doing business as a whole first, and the appropriate combination of parts next. Everyone from the CEO to the delivery truck driver knows the big picture, how he or she fits into it, and why. This revolution is shaped as much by individuals as noted as Deming and others less known, as by corporate risk-takers, or by articles and books like this one, that explore new approaches and new practices.

I am indebted to many people for my own understanding of this new management vision. Lewis Veraldi stands out. He, and many others whom he inspired and who supported him, proved that there was a far better way to go about our work, that we had it in ourselves as assembly-line workers, engineers, or designers to excel in ways we had somehow lost touch with. Under his tutelage, in 1986, the Taurus and Sable cars rolled off Ford's production lines, the culmination of a $3 billion bet-the-house gamble for the company and in some ways for the country. Veraldi died in 1990 at age 56, before he could make his full impact on the company to which he was dedicated and to the society around him.

I first met Veraldi during the early years of the Taurus project. His enthusiasm for his work was palpable. He liked to depict his new managerial style as a large circle on a wall chart. "I'm in the middle," he would say, "and all around are the special departments fanning out. Now what's important here is that anyone on that chart can talk to anyone else without having to think about departmental walls." Veraldi's vision of a seamless operation was embodied in Team Taurus. While he would never have put it this way, he had rediscovered the link between the subjective human side (thoughts, feelings) and the measurable results (parts, components) in the teaming he induced.

Veraldi's approach turned Ford's fortunes around. But his real contribution was larger. It pointed the United States to a new management vision apart from the Tayloristic principles that were so deeply ingrained. Today, Ford is not alone in forging a new management style, and struggling to adapt to the Japanese challenge. In 1991, GM lost $6–8 billion dollars and announced layoffs of 74,000 people. It now has its back to the wall much as Ford did ten years earlier.

A new management agenda lies ahead. This book explains one piece of that agenda: the weaving together of companywide teams that gather strength by understanding the whole endeavor to which they are connected. This frees them to function independently of the artificial organizational labels and boundaries constructed around them. It also frees them to tap the collective genius of the group rather than be satisfied with simply cementing individually conceived parts into a lesser whole.

Tackling this agenda with a vigor and will of a Lew Veraldi will take the nation a long way toward the national goal of restoring its competitive edge in world markets. It will allow corporate America to mark the end of a 100-year evolution of Tayloristic methods.

A deeper aspect of the new management agenda is briefly alluded to through the quotations introducing each of the five parts constituting this book. Taken from leading figures in artificial intelligence and neural net research, neuroscience, psychology, and organizational behavior, they share a common conceptual foundation with *cross-function* teaming. All treat phenomena holistically and treat the new paradigm of massively parallel process management as more truly representative of organic behavior. These features are central indeed to the functioning of the seamless enterprise.

The chapters themselves are my interpretation of the new management paradigm loosely referred to as Total Quality Management. While the subject is extensive and the volume of literature on the subject growing rapidly, this book represents the first effort by an American author to focus on the phenomenon of *cross functions* as the truly innovative breakthrough of TQM.

Dan Dimancescu
Guest Faculty,
Thayer School of Engineering
Darmouth College
and
President, Technology & Strategy Group
8 Story Street
Cambridge, Massachusetts 02138
(617) 497-1111; Fx (617) 547-2378

THE SEAMLESS ENTERPRISE

PART I

OVERVIEW

The holistic entirety constitutes a dynamic system of transactions.... Integrative actions are continuously insuring that the system operates as a unified whole.

From "Brain, Mind, and Self" by Hadley Cantril with Dr. William K. Livingston, 1966. In *Psychology, Humanism & Scientific Inquiry,* ed. Arthur Cantril, Transaction Books, 1988.

1: A NEW AGENDA

From afar, American corporate headquarters seem to be paragons of the latest and best practices. The image is of flawless delivery of products and services, errorless billing, and state-of-the-art research. This is the way it looks at Basking Ridge, where AT&T is sedately headquartered; at Hewlett-Packard's Palo Alto headquarters; and at American Express's Battery Tower in lower Manhattan. Such companies represent the apogee of American success.

However, what is seen from afar is often only a veneer of "latest and best." Closer observation of many brand-name U.S. corporations reveals organizational structures and management methods that have grown obsolete. Day-to-day work habits are increasingly counterproductive because of overspecialization, narrow departmental loyalties, and excessive administrative controls.

The typical American organizational structure of compartmentalized divisions, departments, and functions stands squarely in the way of effective performance. The price is enormous. I call it the *30 percent factor.* In many companies time-to-market cycles are 30 percent longer than the world's best; costs are 30 percent higher; and quality is 30 percent inferior (often worse). As competing against leaner, more flexible enterprises gets tougher, more companies acknowledge that key areas, such as product quality, cannot be improved without changing design procedures and time-to-market management methods. The challenge is daunting. Improvements ranging from 100 to 1000 percent are necessary to outperform the world's best competitors; 10 percent improvements here and there are not enough.

At the core of today's mainstream practices are two lingering traditions, each antithetical to an emerging set of total quality management practices. One is the Tayloristic legacy of job specialization inherited from generations of scientific management (see Appendix, p. 213). Workers are limited to expertise in their immediate jobs, without understanding the whole system of which they are a part. This runs counter to the total quality vision of workers as self-empowered with statistical process control tools so that they can comprehend and thus improve a complete process, not just isolated parts.

The second tradition is "command and control," inherited from once-innovative techniques developed by Alfred P. Sloan at General Motors during the 1930s. Sloan made the complexity of huge organizations manageable by dividing them into smaller parts, which were in turn subjected to top-down "command and control" through tight financial management. The system rested on a fundamental principle: "he who holds the purse string, commands." Structures that institutionalized this behavior evolved into vertically managed hierarchies. At the bottom, workers with "scientifically" prescribed job descriptions were controlled by rewards and punishments from the next layer up. There could be as many as twenty layers of foremen and executives separating bottom from top. Eventually, the smallest parts of the corporation at the bottom became very narrowly specialized.

In their time these techniques worked wonders. America's post-World War II economic miracle rested squarely on the power of Taylor's disciplined scientific management practices and Sloan's organizational principles. As our productivity exploded, European economic and political dominance withered. But by the 1960s and more clearly during the 1970s problems emerged. Our competitive momentum stalled. It soon became apparent that, as more complex administrative procedures were instituted to get all those specialized parts to work together, the parts grew less and less able to communicate among themselves. Results were harder and harder to achieve "by the book." When unions wanted to slow production, all they had to do was operate by the book. And little got done.

As the formal systems ossified, managers and workers circumvented them. " Dotted line" management ensued: dots and arrows were drawn onto formal organization charts in order to link people together into ad hoc teams that actually got things done. All those dotted lines were an acknowledgment that formal organization charts and the management system did not work. The former usually sat unread on corporate bookshelves or merely filled in space in annual reports.

Steve Stevens, a "shipping receiving distributor" in an electronics parts firm in Waltham, Massachusetts, illustrates dotted line management at work. His job is to pick up orders for components from one department and return with the component ready for assembly into a final product that will be shipped. "I'll give you an example," he said to me one day. "I had to go and pick up stuffing wires set into a cable sheath. I would have to go to Department A and request it to request the wires from Department B. I would then have to wait three days. So most of the time I just go around channels. I skip the forms and do it in a single trip. All the regular system does is push productivity down. It makes shipping late and gets customers mad." And then he added, "The worst is that it makes the workers look bad. We just can't do our work fast."

Times may have changed, but Steve's company has not. It is the 30 percent factor at work. A large majority of American— and indeed many European—corporations are still managed by top-down departmental accountability. The organizational labels are similar: engineering, finance, purchasing, sales, legal, and research and development. Many times plants, sales offices, and laboratories are geographically dispersed.

In this "vertical" management style, individual tasks are often completed in one department or group and then handed off to the next without full appreciation of the whole process. Specialized groups often develop their own professional language, not readily understood by other departments. In other cases, cumbersome administrative procedures are instituted with the sole purpose of managing the transfer of work from one group to another. Organizational chimneys or stove pipes, quickly develop their own narrow reward systems. The resulting allegiance to such departmental chimneys can work at cross-purposes with the company's overall needs.

Such structures not only diminish corporate effectiveness, but also increase remoteness from the end customer. Eventually, of course, there is a price to pay for the failure to communicate and coordinate effectively across organizational barriers. Costs go up. Time and resources are wasted. And as we know from the 1970s and 1980s, customer loyalty shifts swiftly to companies that more closely serve their interests.

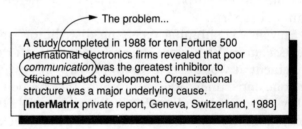

The problem...

A study completed in 1988 for ten Fortune 500 international electronics firms revealed that poor *communication* was the greatest inhibitor to efficient product development. Organizational structure was a major underlying cause.
[**InterMatrix** private report, Geneva, Switzerland, 1988]

Figure 1-1

The solution to this problem (see Figure 1-1) is not more technology, such as costly automation equipment, from our labs. Late in 1988 three academics—Kim Clark, W. Bruce Chew, and T. Fujimoto—published a working paper comparing 29 auto-industry car development projects in the United States, Europe, and Japan. Both the United States and Europe invested three times more engineering hours than Japan to create a car. Average lead times showed the United States and Europe at 50 and 46 months, respectively, versus 35 for the Japanese. The percentages of supplier-designed parts were 15 and 35 percent for the United States and Europe, 52 percent for the Japanese. These were startling numbers because they highlighted the fact that something other than "high-technology" machines, materials, and computers explained the difference in productivity.[1]

A NEW AGENDA

At Hughes Aircraft, D. Kenneth Richardson, President and Chief Operating Officer, frames the dilemma this way: "The focus on functional department accountability and achievement of objectives coupled with the usual layered reward systems all contribute to problems in lateral communications and decision making. The classic functional manager must let go of some of the authority and control over his or her people."[2]

The cost of the impediments raised by this system can be high. Design rework resulting from "throw it over the transom" processes can eat up a significant percentage of a development budget in a complex engineering project. Managers at Boeing Commercial estimate that up to 30 percent of airplane development cost may be attributed to design rework that is built into sequential process methods.

The cost is also measured in lost market share, as GM well knows. Its enormous investments in automation technologies during the decade of the 1980s resulted in a 12 percent decline in North American automotive market share. The French automaker Peugeot was finally forced in 1991 to abandon the U.S. market because of buyer perceptions of inferior quality caused by defects in the 405 model series. Audi, a Volkswagen product, suffered enormously from a troublesome lurch in one car model.

These are not just big-company problems. Smaller companies often think of themselves as "cross-functional" because everyone knows everyone else and knows everything that is going on. But when it comes to working as suppliers to large companies, small firms quickly get caught up in the departmental chimneys of large customer corporations—purchasing (for specifications), accounting (for billing), legal (for contracts), and quality inspection (for defects)—before making contact with the actual customer within the corporation.

Because these cultural and organizational impediments to accepting a new agenda are a legacy of decades of narrowly compartmentalized functions and specialization, there is an enormous reluctance to change them. Even in academe, narrow boundaries and vertical organizational structures are deeply entrenched. The reward systems in business and academe encourage narrow specialization: academics advance by writing scholarly articles in their field; a manager is rewarded for performance in his or her narrow function or department. The blue-chip MBA schools are inadvertently the worst offenders because they attract the scholarly talent most interested in advancing through specialized research. Their students, in turn, are channeled into careers that mirror academic and corporate chimneys. No one "owns" or teaches companywide processes, such as quality, delivery, or cost. "You don't get published in the journals with a topic like that," is a common observation.

THE WORLD OF MBAs

- I asked a class of MBA students at a top-ten business school to list all the vertical functions they would encounter in a large company. "Which chimney would you build a career in?" Finance and marketing headed the list. Lowest on the list was Personnel. None were able to see a career in managing "cross" functions.
- At another top-ten business school, I proposed teaching a course in cross-functional program management. Although the Dean supported the course, no faculty person was interested in promoting it because the course cut across several departments. The course was not implemented.

Breaking this legacy is central to making American firms more competitive. The new paradigm of cross-function management recognizes that *process,* or *how we get things done,* must be treated as a strategic corporate priority. It argues that competition is won by treating all parts of the firm as a single unified whole. This is what makes the emergence of total quality management during the last decade so promising and powerful a methodology. But what is not yet understood is that cross-function management is a vital centerpiece in making TQM a holistic approach to management. It provides a means of unifying actions across complex organizations. Without understanding cross-function methods, TQM cannot be implemented. "TQM is a leadership philosophy, an ability to look at every product and service you provide from everyone's point of view," says Aris Melissaratos, a vice president of the Westinghouse Electric Corporation.[3]

As much as TQM is discussed in the popular press and in an increasing number of books, its principles and key elements remain fuzzy. An example is an article in the bimonthly publication of the American Electronics Association referring to TQM as a "tool" that has been implemented "in manufacturing" by almost one-third of a surveyed group of 311 companies.[4] Such references are highly misleading. TQM is not a tool, although tools and techniques are sub-elements of it. It is a contradiction to suggest that it can be applied within a single chimney such as manufacturing since the goal of TQM is to unify activities across all departmental boundaries, often including suppliers.

In a publicly circulated journal, a brand-name consulting company optimistically heralds its service as going "Beyond Quality." It suggests that "TQM—in practice—can fall short [because] it improves processes at the micro-level, typically within a single function." Given this perceived shortcoming, the same firm offers to redesign a business process to, in its words, go "beyond TQM." How? It "focuses on core, cross-functional processes." This firm not only misrepresents what TQM really is but then goes on to offer a "cross-functional" solution that is actually the essence of TQM.

A fundamentally different approach to management than is conventionally practiced in the United States, TQM's goal is to make the whole greater than its parts. Conventional U.S. management, on the other hand, has rigidified into being a simple sum of parts.

The TQM model is composed of five principal management elements: vision setting, strategy definition, policy deployment, results through bottom-up quality methods, and process control through cross-functional management (see Figure 1-2).

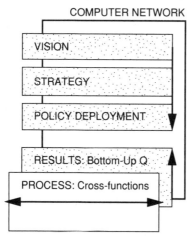

Figure 1-2 The holistic TQM model and cross functions

It is a structured interplay of information flows analogous to the nerve system of a firm. Top-down directives on vision, strategy, and policy emanate from senior management and are disseminated companywide; bottom-up feedback on day-to-day operations is generated by workers using statistical process control tools; and lateral cross-function flows linking all vertical chimneys together are instituted to ensure consistency of execution companywide. Since all are dependent on an open system of communication companywide, a sixth factor comes into play as an underlying element: computer networks as the physical manifestation of the nerve system. In this perspective, the TQM model represents a holistic system necessary to respond to customer-driven markets, continuous improvement processes, and horizontal concurrency of task flows.

Cross-function methods have a common overriding purpose: to encourage communication laterally across a corporation. It is inseparable from TQM. Because it is the key to weaving a *process* laterally across the firm so that all parts function in unison and not at cross purposes, it is inseparable from TQM. Although the term *cross-functional* is frequently used simply to describe multidisciplinary teaming, the real practice and methods of "cross-function" management are new to most American firms.

To survive in markets that demand more efficient performance, American businesses are challenged to fill a vacuum in current management practices: managing horizontally *across* divisions, departments, and suppliers. Not to change will sustain wasteful habits that eventually become debilitating. Tackling the 30 percent factor through more holistic management practices will do more to restore vitality to the U.S. economy than any other single initiative, public or private.

Notes

Chapter 1

1. Kim B. Clark, W. Bruce Chew, and T. Fujimoto, "Product Development in the World Auto Industry: Strategy, Organization, and Performance," April 1988, Harvard Business School (Division of Research) working paper.

2. Speech at the University of Southern California, Los Angeles, January 1991.

3. "Corporate Lessons in Campus Quality," *The New York Times*, 4 August 1991, education section, p. 28.

4. As reported in *Update*, American Electronics Association, June–July 1991.

2: CROSS FUNCTIONS

Cross-functional management addresses problems associated with sequential hand-offs and chimney-like structures by creating a new category of functions that threads across traditional departmental boundaries—thus the term *cross-function*. The term "cross function" is used by the author to distinguish it from the expression "cross-functional." The latter is used in the U.S. business literature as a general reference to multidisciplinary teams. These are usually collages of vertical chimneys, not a recognition of a new horizontal category of functions. The concept of a cross function adds a critical dimension to Total Quality practices by linking divisional and departmental activities through horizontal communication. This dimension is what is missing in many Western companies' conception of TQM.

Initial corporate efforts in quality management generally consist of statistical process control (SPC) methods advocated by technical staff close to manufacturing activities on the shop floor. In a typical firm, this means that the application of traditional

CROSS FUNCTIONS

statistical quality methods is limited to specific organizational chimneys, principally manufacturing and engineering. This may produce beneficial and immediate results within those "chimneys." But it is no guarantee of corporate improvement because other departments, untutored in quality techniques, can drag the whole enterprise down to their own level of incompetence. A vivid example is that of a hospital capable of performing superb surgery but not able to provide adequate postoperative care. The patient may survive the operation but not the recovery. A more conventional case might be a computer vendor that makes an excellent machine but has a service department with a poor reputation. This situation was a major cause of Wang Laboratories' rapid downturn. During the mid-1980s it was readily apparent to its user community that service calls were poorly administered, parts were not always available, and billing was peripatetic. Because service rates were so high, it was not unusual for service representatives to moonlight their personal service to Wang users at cheaper rates off the books.

A common remedy is to establish a *new* chimney entitled "Quality" to administer quality operations companywide (see

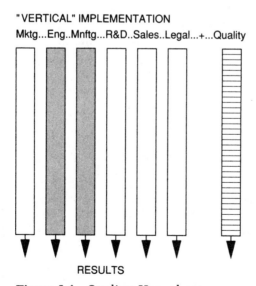

"VERTICAL" IMPLEMENTATION

Mktg...Eng..Mnftg...R&D..Sales..Legal...+...Quality

RESULTS

Figure 2-1 Quality: How about a Quality Department?

Figure 2-1). All this does, however, is to add another organizational barrier. With it come problems of getting other departments to buy in. Some may, but others may do so reluctantly or not at all. One reason is that the new chimney does not have the prestige or authority of Research and Development, Finance, or Engineering. Many times what the "Quality Department" believes others should do is taken more as a hindrance than a benefit. It is a bit like the oft repeated joke: "I'm from the government and I'm here to help you," which becomes "I'm from 'Quality' and I'm here to help you."

WHAT ARE CROSS FUNCTIONS?

Cross functions are introduced into a company for the purpose of optimizing performance companywide. Without them, performance, in the eyes of the customer or shareholder, is sub-optimized because specialized departments plan and execute policy insulated from one another. One department's activities may work at cross-purposes with those of anothers. Without cross-function management, things such as quality, cost, delivery, characteristics are rarely optimized. The most common example is the cost involved in servicing an automobile for a defect covered by a warranty. The customer wastes time taking the car to be serviced. The car company loses because parts must be replaced, mechanics paid, and future goodwill lost with a customer. Warranty control is an example of a cross function with the goal of minimizing cost and maximizing customer satisfaction.

A DEFINITION

Japanese experts define cross function as "a management process designed to encourage and support interdepartmental communication and cooperation throughout a company—as opposed to command and control through narrow departments or divisions. The purpose is to attain such company-wide targets as quality, cost, and delivery of products and services by optimizing the sharing of work."

From a definition by the *Japan Union of Scientists and Engineers* (JUSE), Tokyo 1988

CROSS FUNCTIONS

The objective of a cross function is to focus on critical process issues that cut across the whole enterprise. These issues include such things as *quality, cost control, and delivery* but also a variety of others that are equally important such as *purchasing, personnel training, research, and information management.* Each is treated as a horizontal cross function. This stress on process, or "how" to align all the activities of the company, complements traditional results-minded management, which is concerned with "what" is produced and in what quantities.

Another way to express the difference is by thinking of "results" as the responsibility of vertical divisional, departmental, or functional chimneys. Sales generates revenues. Engineering produces designs. Manufacturing builds things. Finance manages money. Legal drafts and reviews contracts. Process, on the other hand is horizontal. It focuses on how Sales, Engineering, Manufacturing, Finance, Legal, and other vertical functions can work together to satisfy a customer requirement. Underlying this approach is a belief that attending to how one does things is a precondition to building customer confidence. Market share and profitability follow. The combination of vertically managed results and cross-function process control is at the heart of any effort to implement the TQM paradigm (see Figure 2-2).

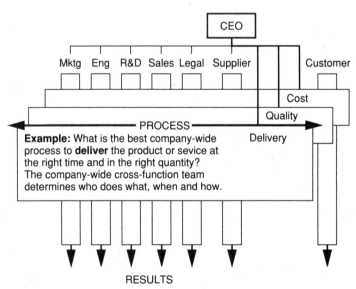

Figure 2-2 Cross-function "process teams"

Commenting on the evolution of cross-function management in Japan between 1960 and 1990, professor Kozo Koura uses a warp and woof image to describe the integration of cross-function techniques and vertical functions.

> 1. Vertical management, management based on passing orders down a "line structure," was dominant thirty years ago. Because of this, the communications and cooperative systems between departments were insufficient, and horizontal management was not effective enough to solve company-wide problems. When it came to such functions as "quality assurance," for example, the roles and duties of each division were not clear and appropriate authority was not properly delegated.
> 2. It was necessary to create a structure which, like a piece of cloth, is woven together in two directions. The vertical is the 'warp', and the horizontal is the 'woof'. The two make for a productive system of coordination between all company-wide parts and set the stage for more efficient management.[1]

In Japan, 30 years of experimentation has resulted in a pattern of management that operates in both vertical and horizontal dimensions. This approach, although it is perceived as mirroring uniquely Japanese cultural traits, is replicable in almost any corporate setting. It is interesting to note that what the Japanese recognized as a competitive failing 30 years ago is exactly what ails many Western companies today.

Cross-function activities are woven through the vertical structure of a firm by teams with companywide divisional or departmental representation. A "cost" process team, for example, will not consist of specialists in cost accounting or finance, but of line representatives with direct responsibility to produce results within each of the vertical chimneys that may have an impact on cost control throughout a company. This is an important distinction. *Line people take on two responsibilities*: to manage vertical functions as well as to coordinate process horizontally.

In some cases the membership may cut diagonally through different layers of hierarchy. The CEO might sit on the same cross-function team as a key account sales manager or a purchasing administrator.

CROSS FUNCTIONS

It must be emphasized that cross-function management is not conventional two-boss matrix management with vertical functions on one axis and project teams on another. Neither is it a patchwork of disciplines brought together as an ad hoc team. It is a deliberate effort to build a structure and a process that **encourage communication horizontally** across the organization. The emphasis on "lateral communication" is crucial. It is the core to what makes a firm seamless — or not.

QUALITY AT AT&T

In AT&T the quality renaissance focuses on rediscovering the basics of quality that were largely originated in the former Bell System, and applying modern technology to build a total, seamless process for delivering quality to our customers....

The critical thrust of the Quality Architecture is to establish cross-company interfaces and systems that effectively support marketplace requirements, and to build understanding of, and responsibility for, quality among all employees. We endeavor to create a shared vision of quality throughout AT&T.

Laurence C. Seifert, VP Engineering, Manufacturing, and Production Planning, AT&T, 1987

Cross-function teaming creates *a corporate whole greater than the sum of its parts*. The analogy in sports terms, whether it is rugby, basketball, or football, is a team working in sync rather than as a collection of solo self-centered stars. As with the Boston Celtics, a team that shuns solo superstars, the focus is on creating strategies and plays that use individual players, coaches, and support staff in the service of the whole team. In corporate terms it means mapping relationships and "plays" between research and development, marketing, engineering, sales, distribution, suppliers, and customers. Firms like Compaq or Sun Microsystems have won market share in a relatively short time by performing as seamless teams. Sun has extended the teaming process to include large networks of external suppliers. As on a winning sports team, the total corporate effort optimizes individual departmental strengths for the benefit of its customers.

The payoff is tangible. Companies introducing cross-function management (CFM) practices as part of more comprehensive TQM programs see dramatic improvements in performance. They eliminate expensive administrative overhead and redundant activities, which in turn reduces product development time cycles, lowers costs, and increases customer satisfaction. And teaming individuals together across departments accelerates innovation because good ideas are shared across a wider set of organizational boundaries.

A SAMPLING OF COST, DELIVERY, AND QUALITY BENEFITS RESULTING FROM HORIZONTAL TEAMING

AT&T

Cost of repair of a circuit pack: reduced 40%
Total process time for a PBX: reduced 46%
Defects: reduced 30% to 87% on components

Hewlett-Packard Instruments Division

Manufacturing cost: reduced 45%
Development cycle: reduced 35%
Field failure rates: reduced 60%
Scrap and rework: reduced 75%

Deere & Company

Development costs: 30% savings
Development time: 60% less
Inspectors: reduced by 2/3

Source: *Institute for Defense Analyses*

CFM IS PROCESS MANAGEMENT — NOT CRISIS MANAGEMENT

The temptation in traditionally managed companies is to treat problems as "crises." "Someone has screwed up again," is the frequent reaction of a manager. The management process is never the problem. Grumbling that "Heads will bounce on this one," the manager will jump into the fray, give orders, talk about incompetence, and, if the problem is serious enough, penalize someone. "You've got to kick ass," is the way an automotive plant manager once put it to me. He may think that the problem is resolved, yet nothing has really changed. The system is the same and employees are a bit more weary. The next time they will do it "just by the book" to get back at the manager. And things still will not work as well as they might. This is not process management.

Managing process by cross functions takes the whole system into account by mapping all the relationships necessary to efficiently achieve a goal. A crisis is generally viewed as a defect of the process. Of course, a late delivery of a product, incorrect billing, or defects in a product are immediate problems needing prompt resolution, but it is understood that behind these problems is a larger failure. Heads rolling and a lot of shouting are rarely viewed as solutions. Improving the *process* with the help of all team players is.

This is one reason that cross-function teams are not composed of staff people tucked away in corporate planning offices. Staff are too removed from the people who know and live with a process. The most effective cross-function teams consist of line people with day-to-day responsibilities taken from across a company's divisions, departments, suppliers, or customers. Through such teams, one part of the company must take the needs of another into account and must treat this other part much as its own customer. Boeing Commercial uses the term "cosuppliers" for each of the players on a cross-functional team.

This systemic perspective also permits product development teams to treat the totality of a product's full life cycle from inception to disposal. This is particularly important in drawing customer needs into the complete evolution of a product. In addition, it responds to growing pressures to address such environmental issues as toxic disposal early in the design phases. All of this cannot be done without bringing all the key players to the table on a single team.

CONTINUOUS LEARNING

This style of seamless management calls for careful documentation of *all* critical process events and activities that link a company-wide team. The initial purpose, like the lowering of the water level to reveal rock shoals, is to identify barriers to information sharing across departments and to more easily target non-value-adding activities. But if the analysis of how things get done company-wide is well documented, it can also become an important corporate learning resource. When people advocate the development of a "learning organization," they often overlook the substantial value that comes from documenting *process activities* in ways that are easily communicable to the next round of players. Cross-function management puts a premium on careful documentation. A firm managed this way has a running start on traditionally managed competitors that must reinvent ad hoc teams, procedures, and data requirements.

Soul of a New Machine, a best selling book by Tracy Kidder, described a very successful effort by a design team to create a new computer product at Data General, a Massachusetts computer company. Yet because the effort was ad hoc, it left no tracks. There was little learning transferred to the next project cycle, and the parent company did not use the team's experience as a jumping-off point for the next project. The team's members, burned out from the pressure to succeed, disbanded. Some members left the firm feeling exploited and unrewarded. This was not a case of corporate learning from prior experience.

In contrast, at Sony, continuity of teamwork is central to product development. Instead of short-sighted management of each product development cycle, Sony emphasizes a product evolution through continual refinements, each of which provides entry into a new market segment. The Sony Walkman, for example, evolved over ten years into more than one hundred eighty variations. The iteration processes, and the technologies involved were meticulously documented. In the next iteration all the company had to do was to add or eliminate minor features to tap a new market segment. In this manner it was able to get new products quickly to market and outpace its competitors. "It may not have been elegant wiring inside," says an ex-employee of Sony, "but it got us to the next round fast." Aiwa, Sony's closest competitor, was able to put only half as many Walkman-styled variations on the market during the same period, Toshiba one-tenth the number.

Such a management model recalls Kozo Koura's "warp and woof" imagery. A tight communication network is developed

21

CROSS FUNCTIONS

linking all parts of the corporation. The trick, of course, is to learn how to discipline the process so that randomness is not the result. What one wants is controlled "chaos": a process that is replicable, ever improving, with the potential for unexpected innovations.

CHAOS AND RANDOMNESS

At the risk of oversimplification, I like sometimes to suggest the difference between chaos and randomness by comparing the behavior of commuters dashing through a train station at rush hour with the behavior of a large terrified crowd. The activity of the commuters resembles chaos in that although an observer unfamiliar with train stations might think people were running every which way without reason, order does underlie the surface complexity: everyone is hurrying to catch a specific train. The traffic flow could be rapidly changed simply by announcing a train track change. In contrast, mass hysteria is random. No simple announcement would make a large mob become cooperative.

"The Psychology of Perception," by Walter J. Freeman, *Scientific American*, February 1991

A beneficial by-product of three-way top-down, bottom-up, and lateral flows is the controlled chaos as people and information cross paths. It is a potential well of serendipitous innovation from unexpected connections between people and overlapping information sources that would otherwise be organizationally insulated from one another in what is sometimes characterized as command and control or machine theory management.

THE ELECTRONIC NERVE SYSTEM

Because communication is the basis of TQM, electronic tools are a hidden resource. Computer and communication networks are analogous to a nerve system. They can react to impulses, transmit data, and filter messages throughout a system. Cross-function concepts such as "simultaneity," "concurrency," and "parallel processing," are facilitated and implemented through electronic means. This makes networks particularly well suited as a support system for holistic TQM practices. But for reasons that are different in their origin, electronic facilitation of TQM practices has been inhibited in both Japan and the United States.

In Japan, companies have been averse to desk-top terminals. One reason is that terminals have, until recently, been unwieldy machines with complex keyboards because of complex Kanji (Chinese) characters. A minimum of 2500 are needed to read a newspaper; 50,000 are part of the day-to-day language. Powerful and cheaper workstations have now solved this problem. However, another inhibitor is the social culture of companies. Face-to-face communication is a preferred method of getting things done. Floor layouts are open, with desks normally pushed together to encourage direct contact. In addition, lateral communication between "departments" is far easier if only because employees are job-rotated between vertical chimneys. A common companywide language is derived in this way. All of this has made desktop computers and electronic networks less ubiquitous than in the United States.

COMPUTERS AT TOYOTA

Taiichi Ohno, the inventor of kanban (JIT) methods among other things at Toyota, "preferred to have daily process flow information proceed not by computer orders but by the exchange of kanban for the simple reason that 'the real world doesn't always go according to plan....' It even seemed to Toyota managers that letting final assembly regulate previous processes kept inventories at lower levels than were possible with the best MRP [material resource planning] systems, because they removed processing to a distant point—the central computer."

Michael Cusumano, *The Japanese Automobile Industry,* Harvard University Press, 1985, p. 298

In the United States, the cultural obstruction is a legacy of a centralized, top-down command and control management model. When commercial computers first appeared, this created a bias toward centralized 'head office' mainframe computers as the *visionary* solution to corporate information management. This, we now recognize, is a flawed vision. It was aggravated as competing computer vendors started to offer distributed systems to specialized departments. Engineers bought DEC and Hewlett-Packard; front office "bean counters" wanting centralized financial and administrative controls bought IBM. And the machines did not talk together. Neither did the advocates of different computing solutions. By the mid-1980s networks were jury-rigged patchworks of competing vendors' equipment.

Yet, despite these problems, there is clearly a basis for integrated networks to support a seamless style of management. This may be especially true of the United States. With the rapid proliferation of desktop IBM-PCs (and compatibles), MacIntoshes, and high-powered workstations, many companies now count three terminals for every two workers. The desktop computer will be the focal point of networking solutions. Even in Japan the overall count is one terminal for three employees and growing fast. Laptops are popping up in greater and greater numbers. Toshiba's laptop plant in Ome, near Tokyo, has 4000 employees, each equipped with a laptop. All of them are networked to exchange information. Such ubiquity and the rapid evolution of universal communication standards means that systems can now be designed to support the organizational and management architecture of the TQM model.

Because of its affinity for developing and using computer technology, the United States is in a more advantageous position to develop innovative electronic support systems. An example of this affinity at work centers on a new method of developing new product characteristics with Quality Function Deployment (QFD) matrices (Chapter 9, *Needs/Solutions*, p. 118). Although QFD techniques and matrices were invented in Japan during the early 1970s and widely propagated, no single Japanese company developed a practical software application to ease the making of these charts. But within a few years of first learning about Quality Function Deployment in 1984, Ford Motor Company had developed a commercially available software application as well as an expert system for internal use. A software company in Ohio, International TechneGroup (ITI), created a commercial product now widely sold. And Rockwell International spent in excess of $1 million to create a QFD application of its own. This single example suggests the beginning of a U.S. learning curve that will accelerate into an electronic nerve system for the TQM model (see discussions of groupware in Chapter 14). To date, the vision of an electronically "integrated enterprise" remains elusive even though all of the technological solutions are available to achieve it. The reason is a compartmentalized management style standing in the way.

A LAST WORD...

By recognizing the need to manage complex information flows, the TQM model has emerged as a primary alternative to a still prevalent command and control, top-down American model of management. This new cross-function management style, first developed in the 1960s by Toyota and Komatsu, was a breakthrough in moving toward a truly seamless organizational fabric. The vertical elements retained responsibility for results and the horizontal for managing companywide processes. The value of this approach is only now being recognized in the West, where, with the support of networked computer technologies, cross-function management has enormous potential to effect change. But from the 1960s to date, the methods remained largely insulated from view and ignored by Western firms.

Notes

Chapter 2

(The term "cross function" as I use it does not have the same meaning as "cross-functional." The latter is used in U.S. business literature as a general reference to multidisciplinary teams. These are usually collages of vertical chimneys, not a new horizontal category of functions.)

1. Kozo Koura, Lecturer at Aoyama Gakuin University, *Survey and Research in Japan Concerning Cross-Function Management*, Unpublished manuscript abstract, 1990.

3: THE INNOVATORS

In 1961, Japan's entire auto industry exported 14,000 cars to the United States. (About the same number the U.S. exported to Japan in 1990.) Jokes about Japanese cars being chain driven, poorly designed, and inferior in quality abounded among derisive American auto company executives and workers. At Toyota, however, executives looked to export markets as the key to the company's long-term success and profitability. But if the company was to enter export markets, they also understood well, rusting bodies and lackluster designs would never get them there. Quality and performance standards would have to be improved dramatically.

Analyzing the hurdles in their path, they determined that poor coordination between vertically managed departments and large number of suppliers was stalling quality improvement efforts. "The cooperation of suppliers was central to any future success,"[1] notes professor Kozo Koura. Unlike the Detroit big three auto manufacturers, Toyota relied far more heavily on external suppliers for structural parts and components. This put added pressure on company planners to shorten and improve the product development cycle as the stepping stone to world markets. To do this Toyota needed better ways of linking internal departments and suppliers. This would permit greater numbers of model changes to be offered customers. And in turn, their feedback could be more quickly introduced into new models. As Koura points out, also, Toyota "would gain from having continuous feedback from the market against which to improve their product."

Toyota's strategy meant that markets would be won more by focusing on management "process" than by relying on capital-costly investments in high-technology automation. Constant improvement of quality *across* departmental and supplier boundaries was essential. The formula turned into a winner as sales volume, profitability, or a glance at consumer reports ratings will tell. According to *Fortune* magazine Toyota sits on $22 billion in cash, a sum the magazine deems large enough to buy both Ford and Chrysler at current stock prices.

In Japan Toyota controls 43 percent of the market, and in the U.S. annual unit sales reached a rate of 1 million units. Worldwide its rate of car sales pushed it into third place behind GM and Ford. GM, in contrast, left its hierarchical management methods almost untouched for more than four decades and relied exclusively on automation technology as its competitive resource. GM's North American share of the car market has eroded steadily, while world sales have dropped by about 10 percent over a five-year period from 1986 to 1991.

One of the primary organizational breakthroughs to propel Toyota was the invention of *a new category of companywide functions*. These complemented conventional departmental functions structured as vertical chimneys reporting upward to a CEO. This innovation was akin in magnitude to changes engineered half a century earlier by Henry Ford. The new **cross functions** focused on companywide processes such as meeting customer quality requirements, controlling costs, and meeting deliveries. By April 1962 Toyota had identified thirteen cross functions. A year later the number had jumped to twenty-one. This proved unwieldy, and ten years later the number fell back to six. By 1990 it had leveled off to ten.

TOYOTA'S CORPORATEWIDE CROSS FUNCTIONS

1 Quality	6 Personnel
2 Cost	7 Training
3 Research	8 Safety & Sanitation
4 Production Techniques	9 Information Systems
5 Purchasing	10 TQC Promotion

Each cross function is overseen by a corporate team made up of senior *line* managers. Their job is to design work process blueprints by clearly defining methods and techniques of lateral communication between each of their chimneys. Because each corporate team "owns," or is empowered with the responsibility to design the management process, it serves as a *companywide knowledge team* in the particular functional area. Together these teams have an intimate understanding of the firm's capabilities as a total system. They constitute the CEO's eyes and ears on how things are done and where improvements can be strategically targeted. The results, coupled with a commitment to total quality and its own internal inventions such as just-in-time and kanban, cannot be stated more simply than in *Fortune* magazine's 1991 description of Toyota—30 years after it first determined to implement a "system of cross-function management"—as the best car maker in the world.

By the end of the period 1960 to 1990, almost all major Japanese firms from cosmetic, to tent rental, to semiconductors applied some variation of these methods to their operations. Similar results were exhibited in the Japanese software industry as it applied "manufacturing" quality techniques to the software engineering process. At a Tokyo conference on software quality in February 1989, American attendees from major U.S. firms were startled to find quality standards, measured in defects per thousands of lines of code in large-scale projects, to be one or two orders of magnitude better than their own.

For Japan, the cumulative effect of these managerial innovations with a disciplined focus on effective process management was not only to strengthen its competitive ability in world markets but to allow its economy to ride out the shock of sudden sky-rocketing energy prices and later the weakening of the dollar.

THE AMERICAN STORY

With the exception of a few American firms such as Cummins Engine (influenced by its partner Komatsu during the early 1980s) in Columbus, Indiana, Ford Motor and its Team Taurus (with its own partner Mazda), Kodak in Rochester, N.Y., and Hewlett Packard (which worked closely with its own Japanese partner Yokogawa Electric), these cross-function management innovations failed to capture the interest of American managers or the business schools training them.

Ford's Taurus story, written about at length by various academic and business writers,[2] is important for two reasons. It demonstrated the ability of an American firm to adopt cross-function teaming methods and, for the first time, to meet customer needs. Subsequent to the successful introduction of the Taurus and Sable models, Ford instituted a program designed to streamline its product development process. Operating under the name Concept-to-Customer, it had as a principal mission to tackle the communication problem endemic to an organization built around vertical chimneys. That program was renamed World Class Timing. The goal is to reduce development cycles from 60 months down to 48 months, a target achieved by Toyota and other Japanese auto manufacturers in the mid-1980s and now closer to 36–40 months.

A NEW EXPERIMENT...

Boeing Commercial's "777" airplane program launched in 1990, may be the Team Taurus of the 1990s. As an experiment in cross-function management, the company instituted a process it termed Concurrent Product Definition. The goal was to make two of its long-standing fiefdoms, Engineering, which designs an aircraft, and Operations, which assembles it, partners from the start rather than separate entities functioning at arm's length. The new process would treat them as members of fully integrated design or assembly teams.

In addition, Boeing's normal design approach was linear. One step completed by one engineering discipline led to the next specialized discipline and a new step. Known by everyone at Boeing as the over the wall approach, it was considered a basic cause of a costly and time-consuming design change and rework problem. An in-house diagram from Boeing (see Figure 3-1) illustrates its view of the old system at work.

The 777 project set out to break those chimneys down and with them decades of habits, rewards, cliques, and competing terminologies. Design Build Teams (DBTs) consisting of multi-disciplinary specialists, many to be colocated at single sites, were the principal mechanism for doing this. Concurrency would replace sequential planning. For the 777, all the internal workings and human relationships within this structure would have to be

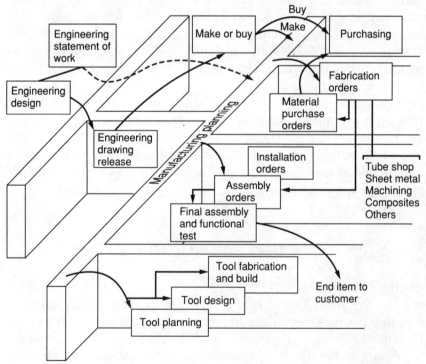

Figure 3-1 Business as usual—product definition and manufacture

reworked to make them function as a horizontal team and not a patchwork of independent specialists. The company gave itself four years to achieve the end goal of fusing 5 million discrete parts into a certified, saleable aircraft. As Alan Mulally, Vice President of Engineering for the 777, put it, "The goal is to build the customer-preferred airplane." The fuse started burning the day aircraft delivery was promised to its first two paying clients: All Nippon Airways and United Airlines. UAL's order totalling $22 billion for 68 of the new "777" aircraft was the largest ever booked.

Behind the changes being instituted in the 777 program was a realization that traditional sequential planning methods and vertically managed specialized technical disciplines induce enormous waste not only during the development of an aircraft but in its full postproduction lifecycle. The share of wasted labor effort was estimated at 30 to 50 percent of total labor costs (see Figure 3.2). This translated into billions of dollars. In excess of 60 percent of labor costs up through the first one hundred production units was required just to keep up with design changes and error. Thereafter, almost 30 to 50 percent of labor effort was needed to accommodate ongoing design changes and errors outside of required customer and certification changes. Phil Condit, General Manager of Boeing's 777 division translated the cost implications in a videotaped address to employees with the following statistics. "One engineering person out of three exists to fix mistakes made by the other two.... That means that we wasted hundreds of millions of dollars in one year alone." He ended by saying, "the money we save is our future." The message was simple: Something needed to be substantially changed in the way Boeing managed its design process or it would begin to lose business to its European rival, Airbus, which launched its technologically advanced A-340 aircraft in October 1991, or to potential American and Asian competitors.

The 777 would be the means for change. An innovative airplane using new materials and improved technology to lower weight, more efficient engines, and more sophisticated interior configuration designs, it would be designed to be three times more reliable than conventional 747s, which have 13,000 hours of flight between failures. In this manner the cost to a client airline of maintaining and servicing a single 777 airplane would be reduced by three to four times.

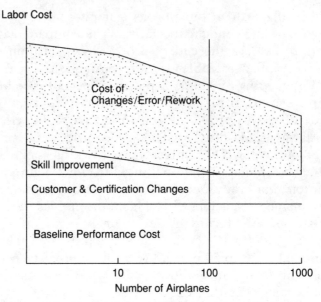

Figure 3-2 Post-production labor cost profile Labor Cost

Boeing put 215 separate DBTs to work; all centered on five major core design teams focused on various major elements of the aircraft such as the body, wing, or final assembly. Also for the first time multiple disciplines would be colocated together. The purpose was not only to break down compartmentalized functions but to induce greater lateral communication and interaction.

"Success of Design Build Teams," wrote Henry Miyatake, a Boeing engineer, "depends on the individual contribution of the key disciplines and the synergistic combination of the team members to improve and refine new methods, generate new ideas, and innovate in an environment of cooperative team effort. This approach uses members from critical technical, business, and manufacturing organizations, pooling their knowledge, experience, and creative energies to meet the team and program objectives."[3] The Boeing experiment is explained in more detail in a subsequent chapter.

CHANGING THE CORPORATE STRUCTURE

Hewlett-Packard is one of the first U.S. firms to experiment with true cross-function teams at the corporate level. One impetus for the change was a product line growing more complex. This demanded far more integration and communication between a decentralized network of divisions. Divided into 85 semiautonomous divisions, HP consolidated late in the 1980s into fifteen. The new Medical Systems Group, for example, merged five business lines in four locations, three in the United States and one in Germany. Another change affected purchasing: all HP divisions were to be supplied by a single internal source for surface mount technology (SMT) on computer chip boards. This would encourage parts commonality and reuse across the company's many product lines.

Once managed on an ad hoc basis, the firm no longer derived competitive advantage. Too many opportunities slipped through the cracks and too many inefficiencies or redundancies resulted. In 1985, a first step was taken by establishing a number of "companywide" councils. Much like Japanese cross-function teams, they were given the responsibility to introduce uniform processes and tighter communication across the company. These councils oversaw Procurement, Productivity, SMT, Manufacturing, or Business Group Research and Development. The purpose of these changes was to formalize horizontal communication.

But like Toyota years earlier, HP found itself inventing more councils than were practical. It soon counted eleven companywide councils. In 1990 a new corporate Product Generation Process Organization became a focal point for all these councils. Its job was to develop "best companywide management and technical processes" for its divisions. Operationally it was divided into two parallel teams, one concentrated on software, the other on hardware.

The vice-president of manufacturing chairs the Hardware Production Generation Team. Its membership of line and staff people is cross-departmental. Not all report directly to the vice-president, but represent departmental "chimneys" such as Distribution, Quality, Finance, Product Generation Process Design, Planning and Management, Product Generation Processes (tools and techniques), Procurement, Technical Education, and Product Definition. As a true cross-function team, it is a major organizational innovation helping Hewlett-Packard overcome its once-praised fragmentation into decentralized engineering and production operations. A year after its organization, it was too soon to tell how effective it would be in redirecting internal operations.

One problem to surface was a tension between individual's responsibilities to meet day-to-day operational obligations against the needs of the Product Generation Team. Day-to-day obligations were winning out as belt-tightening from a computer recession forced attention on short-term needs. But Hewlett-Packard's new cross-function teams clearly staked out new organizational ground based on a recognition that process management was essential to the building of effective communication laterally across the company.

OVERVIEW

In many other companies, such as Stanley Tools or Black and Decker, the move to such integrative styles of management is driven by survival. This, indeed, is what drove Ford's Lewis Veraldi to set a new management style loose on the Taurus project starting in 1980. With customers turning to producers who can meet tighter schedules and provide cheaper products better tailored to their needs, the choice was simple. Change or go out of business.

The Ford, Boeing, and Hewlett-Packard cases discussed above point to the new American agenda. It is helping them, and many others, play catch up with TQM and cross-function management practices. This is ironic given that these practices originated in the United States decades back—not in Japan. However, understanding and studying Japanese innovations and the larger forces behind them gives us a running start in adapting the best of their methods to our own unique requirements and particular corporate personalities.

Notes

Chapter 3

1. Kozo Koura, Lecturer at Aoyama Gakuin University, *Survey and Research in Japan Concerning Cross-Functional Management,* Unpublished manuscript, Tokyo, 1990.
2. An excellent case study of Team Taurus was written by Professor James Brian Quinn of the Amos Tuck School at Dartmouth College with insights contributed by the author.
3. Henry Miyatake, "A Comparison of Two Design/Build Team Concepts," (Boeing Commercial), SME Technical Paper, MM89-02, Dearborn, Michigan.

4: ORIGINS

While the importance of cross-function management is only now beginning to be recognized in America, the ideas underlying the practice are not new. The origins are traced to principles of management taught and practiced by W. Edwards Deming, guru of statistical process control, and to Peter F. Drucker, management consultant and the first to invent what he called the "marketing concept." Deming's ideas go back to the 1930s and Western Electric where he applied them under the tutelage of Dr. Walter A. Shewhart of Bell Labs, the inventor of control charts. Drucker's originate with his writings on the practice of management during the early 1950s.

The significance of Deming and Drucker's works was recognized in Japan after the end of World War II. Hard-pressed business and academic leaders, anxious to build something other than a cheap labor production haven, took their teachings to heart and have since developed them into a powerful management philosophy. It propelled Japanese industry into world leadership in several strategically important

ORIGINS

industrial sectors: automobiles, manufacturing tools and consumer and computer electronics. Software may be next. Meanwhile, mainstream American business, blindsided by the successes of phenomenal consumption growth during the 1950s and
1960s, chose to ignore or apply new practices.

W. EDWARDS DEMING

W. Edwards Deming, starting in the 1950s and for 40 years thereafter, became more and more critical of corporate practices in
America. "The prevailing system of management is destroying our
people—killing their intrinsic motivation, self-esteem, and curios-
ity to learn," he said. "Our recovery requires optimization of the
whole system."[1]

His message was unabashedly holistic: effective work is not
possible without understanding how that work relates to the
whole. Understanding the whole means continuous effort to identify or eliminate any activity that does not add value.

Deming underscored the idea of work process design with the
now famous notion of "PLAN/DO/CHECK/ACT (PDCA)": a cycle
repeated again and again to squeeze out continuous and incre-
mental improvements (see Figure 4-1).

Having learned and first applied his statistical process control
(SPC) techniques in the United States during the 1930s and 1940s
as a student of statistician Walter Shewhart, he argued the importance of applying statistical process control "in *all stages of production* [author's italics], directed towards the most economic
manufacture of a product that is maximally useful and has a
market."[2]

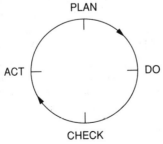

Figure 4-1 "Plan, do, check, act."

Deming found himself far more avidly courted in Japan and other countries than in the United States after World War II. He arrived in Tokyo in 1950 at the invitation of the Japan Union of Scientists and Engineers (JUSE). What followed was a rapid evolution of the tools and techniques necessary for continuous improvement to be institutionalized. JUSE became the focal point of hundreds and eventually thousands of company experiments. Rarely has there been a management laboratory so well focused and coordinated for so long a period. Out of it came an evolution of tools and techniques in Quality Control (QC), and later total Total Quality Control (TQC), and eventually what is now known as Total Quality Management (TQM). A more recent TQM phase opened the door to a new set of practices in cross-functional

HOW IT STARTED

Homer Sarasohn, a young member of General Douglas MacArthur's occupation staff in Japan, recalls deciding with a colleague in 1949 to do something about the inferior materials being delivered by Japanese firms to the military. They would teach a course in American management based on statistical process control methods used by the U.S. Army during World War II. These SPC methods were treated as military secrets during the war years. Sarasohn's idea was not well received by senior staff. "It would create a monster," was the warning. Sarasohn argued that a stronger Japanese economy would prevent the country from being a drain on U.S. taxpayers.

"Finally it went up to MacArthur," he said. As reported to a newspaper by Sarasohn, pro and con sides made 20-minute presentations. "MacArthur got up and began to walk out of the room. As he neared the door, he turned around and told me, 'Go do it.' "

Within a month a textbook was produced by Sarasohn and his colleague, Charles Protzman, on military leave from Western Electric. They both set out to teach it. The course stressed that quality must be a commitment of the entire company, from the management down, and must take precedence over profit. The course also taught that the managers must listen to their workers and gain their trust.... Among Sarasohn's pupils were Sony cofounders Akio Morita and Masaru Ibuka, Matsushita Electric's Masaharu Matsushita, and Mitsubishi Electric's Takeo Kato."

The same training course was taught for the following twenty-five years by various companies.

Adapted from *The Seattle Times/Seattle Post Intelligencer*, July 1, 1990.

management. New techniques were introduced that helped cement communication laterally across corporate boundaries.

The purpose of these quality techniques and tools—which
can be understood in greater depth by reading a growing list of
Japanese and American "how to" books in quality management[3]—
is to empower managers and workers to gather and communicate
concrete facts about the tasks they perform. In their daily work
they can then make intelligent judgments about what might be
wrong, why it went wrong, and how to correct the cause of the
problem. In a continuously reiterated PDCA cycle, this *empowerment* yields enormously productive returns.

These are not the kinds of "tools and techniques" associated
with Harvard Business School, MIT's Sloan School, Amos Tuck at
Dartmouth, Stanford, or Wharton. To them the quality movement
was trade school "stuff," not useful to advancing a scholar's career.
At Harvard Business School's Baker Library, rarely used books by
Deming and others on statistical process control gathered dust on
a shelf in a dark corner of a sub-basement. An important Deming
pamphlet on SPC methods found one day by the author had been
purchased in 1953 and not checked out for 30 years. As a result
the concepts and practices of "continuous improvement" were ignored in the best American business textbooks for almost 35 years
after Deming was embraced in Japan. Americans did not see the
payoffs until the early 1980s, when major corporations rediscovered the quality practices preached by Deming.

PETER F. DRUCKER

"Quality," as Deming defined it, meant maximal usefulness to the
market. While this notion was embraced in Japanese corporations, it was confined to single departments such as manufacturing. Getting departments to cooperate in meeting market needs
remained problematic. This was why another fundamental concept caught the attention of Japanese managers at Toyota. They
gave credit to Peter F. Drucker and his 1956 edition of *The Practice
of Management* as the source of their inspiration.

The purpose of a business, Drucker argued, is "to create customers," an admonition forgotten or ignored by many Western
businesses. Drucker argued that to meet the needs of customers,

the whole business must be delivered to them. This holistic point of view of the practice of management was a cornerstone to the "marketing concept," a term he coined in the early 1950s.[4]

Drucker noted that U.S. firms had a propensity to structure themselves either through federal "divisional" decentralization, or through "functional" decentralization, or combinations of both. This described what Toyota perceived in 1960 to be its own structure—and problem. Hence the significance that Toyota recognized in Drucker's concepts. They meshed perfectly—at least as Japan business visionaries saw it then—with Deming's perceptions of good management practice. Drucker's complementary and equally holistic idea was that the purpose—and the sole purpose of a business—is *to deliver all parts of the enterprise in the service of the customer*. This was not possible with federal and functional compartmentalization. Something else was necessary. Out of this realization was born a managerial innovation focused on integrating the basics of quality control practiced in vertical departments with a system of cross functions.

TQM = Quality Control + Cross-Function Teaming

Visionary Japanese businessmen recognized that cross-function management is a cornerstone to applying Total Quality methods company wide. One married to the other led to the birth of Total Quality Management. The combination is potent. Larry Huston, Quality Manager for Procter & Gamble's research operations, terms the practice of TQM "The Japanese Attack Paradigm." Moving step by step up the value delivery chain, from manufacturing to engineering to design to product conceptualization, the Japanese developed more and more refined techniques to understand customers and to deliver products and services to their expectations. This is translated into Infinitis, Hondas, Sony VCRs, computer chips, motors for copying machines, and liquid crystal displays. Americans buy them by the millions.

"In the United States we have only begun to master quality on the shop floor and are moving quality concepts into engineering," comments Huston. "But the Japanese are now way up the value chain, learning things about what customers really want and how to deliver products and services against those needs. Every time I see a GM car advertisement, I realize how far we still have to go to understand what is meant by being 'customer driven.' " Having come closer to satisfying customer needs, Japanese companies are pushing to revolutionize the distribution of cars. In 1991, Nissan announced plans to produce *one-of-a-kind* cars directly off its *mass* production lines as ordered by its customers. Not only will each one get a "customized" car, but inventories will be reduced.

At the very same time that Toyota and other early innovators, such as Komatsu, were learning from American gurus how to implement "a system of cross-function management" that would deliver on the promise of the marketing concept, U.S. companies accelerated the formal compartmentalization of their functions and corporate structures. One of the first victims was the marketing concept itself. It quickly became a vertical marketing chimney, more and more removed from other operating departments. By the 1980s many marketing operations had become overstaffed activities disconnected from line operations.

Ironically, then, America was the source of management principles that its mainstream business chose, until recently, to ignore. But because of its origins the practice of TQM, which fuses SPC and cross-function methods, is readily transferable to U.S. companies. And it is, at last, gaining a strong U.S. foothold in a rapidly emerging interest in "concurrent engineering."

CONCURRENT ENGINEERING

Concurrent engineering (CE) is America's homegrown experiment with cross-function management. It is being talked about as a new way of breaking across organizational chimneys. Although constrained by the narrow meaning of the word "engineering," the methods and concepts of CE embrace a far broader agenda of concerns. They cover all product development phases and include all departments involved in the product development process, from the beginning to the end of a product's life.

The concept of "concurrency" only recently regained a foothold in American management terminology. Although used in the construction industry for a long time, it took root in a broader industrial community in 1988 when an influential, not-for-profit think-tank, the Institute for Defense Analyses (IDA), was asked by the Department of Defense (DoD) to evaluate a variety of corporate experiments with concurrent engineering carried out during the late 1980s. The purpose was to determine whether these practices could be used to streamline the Department's byzantine acquisition procedures. Not only were cost and time overruns legion, but weapons were not always performing in actual combat (see box). Noting that the acquisition process was predestined to inefficiency both because of its sequential character and by its accounting and auditing bureaucracy, the IDA concluded that "concurrent engineering" would streamline the process.[5]

DOD WEAPONS: DESIGNED BY WHOM FOR WHOM?

I remember the first time I walked into the small, bunkered fire direction center of a 105mm howitzer battery. We were in the field, under combat conditions; the firing charts were set up on a big table; the two specialists and the lieutenant were prepared to brief me on their set-up. As the battalion operations officer, I wanted to know how they ran their show, how fast they could compute firing data and get the rounds on the target some 10,000 meters out in any direction—any direction the infantry asked us to deliver the artillery rounds.

"Lieutenant McGaw, where is your FADAC?" I asked, trying to find out where they had put their computer. He looked at the two fire-direction specialists, and they smiled.

"Sir, it's in the storage container, out in the maintenance tent. We don't use it very often. Too many problems."

"Like what?"

"Every time we move, something happens to it. Breaks down and we have to send it to maintenance."

"How many electric generators do you have?" I asked. McGaw and the other two men laughed.

"One now. We burned one up. Last week we were supporting the 11th ACR, and they were in contact with the enemy for a long time. We were short-handed, as always, and we forgot to go out and switch generators after eight hours of operation. It turned cherry red and stopped running. So we don't have but one generator to run the FADAC. When we reach the eight-hour limit, we have to shut it down and service it. FADAC is just too much trouble to put up with out here in the field."

I didn't like what I heard, but I knew Lt. McGaw had told me the truth. I went around to the other batteries and heard a similar story. It meant that my units were not using a state-of-the-art piece of equipment because it hadn't been designed to hold up under combat conditions. The computer itself was too fragile to withstand the rough movement in a jeep or a five-ton truck, and the generator system that provided the power for the system was unwieldy under the trying conditions of sustained combat. That same generator made so much noise that it signaled the location of the battery to the enemy—even when we put the generators in a revetment and sandbagged them.

We needed the FADAC for the quick computational capability necessary to fire rapidly in any direction. With the FADAC we were more accurate, and we could shift our fields of fire without giving up the reliable weather corrections that the computer could provide. But given the design problems with the system, we had to take very special measures to be able to use it. Every time one of my batteries moved, I flew the FADAC in my helicopter so that it would work when we got there. The generator problem required more discipline among the crews. We couldn't lick the noise problem.

Colonel Pat C. Hoy II (Ret. 1989) From conversations about the Vietnam war with the author.

"The philosophy of concurrent engineering is not new," the report observed. The terms "system engineering," "simultaneous engineering," and "producibility engineering" have been used to describe similar approaches. In fact, varied authors and practitioners have described similar techniques and hundreds of companies have applied them with varying degrees of success. Nevertheless, concluded the IDA, many companies have *not* adopted concurrent engineering because of the "fundamental, wrenching, far-reaching transformations that are required throughout the enterprise." Through concurrent engineering, the study suggested, the DoD's acquisition process could not only be improved but defects and costs in armaments could be greatly reduced.

But beyond making a compelling case for DoD improvements, the most significant contribution of the IDA's study team and its director Robert Winner was in its crisp definition of concurrent engineering. Indeed, it was not really "engineering" they described, but rather a marriage of Deming's continuous improvement quality practices and Drucker's marketing concept.

Concurrent engineering is a systematic approach to the integrated, concurrent design of products and their related processes, including manufacture and support. This approach is intended to cause the developers, from the outset, to consider all elements of the product life cycle from conception through disposal, including quality, cost, schedule, and user requirements....

Concurrent engineering is characterized by a focus on the customer's requirements and priorities, a conviction that quality is the result of improving a process, and a philosophy that improvement of the processes of design, production, and support are never-ending responsibilities of the entire enterprise.[6]

The IDA's study describes the most effective organization as the one that *best delivers the whole enterprise in the service of the customer*. This sounds a lot like Drucker's marketing concept. The IDA adds that the full product life cycle must be taken into account: *"up and through disposal."* In an age of environmental sensitivity, the IDA acknowledges that the customer also includes the general public, which is affected by toxic by-products and waste. This puts an additional premium on getting the early design concepts right and introduces new requirements for products and services. Not just the end user's needs must be considered but also the social or environmental cost.

The IDA's work, while it has yet to affect deep institutional changes in the DoD's acquisition process, has brought a new vocabulary and awareness into the industrial mainstream. Some changes are significantly visible. The DoD has authorized large contracts to develop complex software applications that support cross-department concurrent engineering. The IDA had already initiated studies and reports on what it termed United Life Cycle Engineering (ULCE) to determine appropriate applications of "software technology to facilitate a multi-functional team approach to product design and development process." Another example is the Computer-aided Acquisition and Logistics Support (CALS) initiative established to develop sophisticated cross-disciplinary data management tools.[7] (See Addendum.) In addition, the DoD and other federal agencies, such as NASA, now require contractors to demonstrate that a project is managed "concurrently."

Whether a new cross-functional management style will indeed emerge from these requirements is not known. What it really is remains unexplained by agencies requiring CE as a contractual condition. After the author tracked down NASA's contract officer in charge of concurrent engineering, the officer admitted not knowing what concurrent engineering really entailed. Some observers worry that the requirement will simply create another layer of administrators.

A MERGING OF ROADS

The sudden blossoming of interest in concurrent engineering marks an important turning point for American enterprises. Innovations traced back to Deming, Drucker, and their professional peers are finding a home once again in the United States. This recognition signals the coming of a period of experimentation that, if successful, will restore vitality to the competiveness of American products and services in world markets.

Notes

Chapter 4

1. Andrea Gabor, *The Man Who Discovered Quality*, Random House, New York, 1991.
2. "Statistical Techniques in Industry as a National Resource," Dr. W. Edwards Deming, Bureau of Industrial Statistics, Calcutta, 1952.
3. There are many books on quality management. An example of a recent one outlining the seven new tools, is *Management for Quality Improvement*, Shigeru Mizuno, Ed., Productivity, Cambridge, Massachusetts, 1988. It is interesting to note that it was first written in Japanese in 1979 and took eight years to reach the United States.
4. Peter F. Drucker, *Management—Tasks, Responsibilities, Practices*, Harper & Row, New York, 1974 ed.
5. Robert Winner, et al., *The Role of Concurrent Engineering in Weapons Acquisition*, Institute for Defense Analyses, Report R-338, December 1988.
6. Ibid, p.11.
7. Computer Acquisition and Logistic Support (CALS), established by the Department of Defense (DoD) in 1985, is a DoD/Industry strategy for the transition to automated interchange of technical data, and to process improvements enabled by automation and integration.

PART II

NUTS & BOLTS

Parallel refers to the quality of having many processes go on at the same time: as people walk and talk at the same time, they very likely carry out large numbers of concurrent, mostly unconscious, mental processes. *Distribute* refers to the quality of not being localized: in traditional computers, items of information are stored in particular places, cleanly separated from one another; in neural nets, information is spread out (in principle, a new piece of learning might involve changes everywhere).

From "One AI or Many?" by
Seymour Papert In *Daedalus,* Winter, 1988

5: THE NEW RULES

For TQM and cross-function ideas to flourish, several new rules need to be widely understood by managers and workers. Although introduced in earlier chapters, each is explained in a more complete and systemic way.

The first rule is that product and service requirements are **customer driven**. Doing only what the producer thinks best is no longer viable in markets crowded with competitors. The second rule is **continuous process improvement** or the steady monitoring and correction of problems as they occur. Standing still is not a competitive strategy. The third rule is **concurrency**, or the managing of work activities to include downstream concerns early on. This leads not only to improved lateral communication, but to shorter development cycle time, and to greater quality of work. These new rules frame the competitive challenges of the 1990s.

When IBM released the PC-Jr., a small, cheaply priced computer, it thought it had a winner. Unfortunately, IBM overlooked the most basic rule. No one had asked the potential buyer if he or

THE NEW RULES	Lo		Hi
Rate your company's capability on a scale of:	1	to	10
Customer-driven quality	|——————| |————————|
Continuous improvement	|——————| |————————|
Concurrency	|——————| |————————|

RULE #1: Customer-driven quality

she really wanted a machine with the features of the PC-Jr. Particularly bothersome, it turned out, was a keyboard with hard-to-press buttons. The PC-Jr. was not a customer-driven product in the most commonly understood meaning of the term: meeting the needs of an end user such as a PC buyer. In this regard IBM is far from alone. An example familiar to many is passengers changing from one plane to another at "hub" airports. The system works well for the "producer," the airline, but not for the harried customer.

A broader understanding of customer-driven quality looks at the customer not only as the end user of a product or service, but as whoever is next in performing a task. This greatly expands the concept and has significant ramifications for the product-development process.

Whatever the context, defining a customer's needs and requirements is a complex task. A financial company teaching "quality" to its employees defined the process as a negotiation. Others call it an "art"; to some it is a "science." From a cross-function point of view, the key is how well customer requirements are communicated up and down the value-creation chain. Effective gathering and communicating of customer needs can also play an unexpectedly important role in stimulating employee morale.

WHERE MARKETING STARTED

Peter Drucker, who invented the "marketing concept" during the 1950s, describes it as the fundamental purpose of corporate activity:

> *There is only one valid definition of business purpose: to create a satisfied customer. It is the customer who determines what the business is. Because it is its purpose to create a customer, any business has two and only these two — basic functions: marketing and innovation.*
>
> *Actually marketing is so basic that it is not just enough to have a strong sales force and to entrust marketing to it. Marketing is not only much broader than selling, it is not a specialized activity at all. It is the whole business seen from the point of view of its final result, that is, from the customer's point of view. [1954]*

The customer is often the last person thought of. In one case early in the 1980s a vessel was delivered to the U.S. Navy with its engine rotation designed completely opposite to the rotation of the transmission. Ford's Edsel, Du Pont's Corfam, DEC's Rainbow, and GM's Alliante were all big-buck investments designed and managed by large, fragmented organizations that lost touch with the marketplace. Understanding the customer's point of view is essential if a company is to avoid serious penalties. Basic ideas for product designs formulated early in the life cycle of a product will determine 70 to 80 percent of the eventual costs built into that product. This means that any failure to understand the customer early on can only be remedied at geometrically higher costs later. And if, as is increasingly common, one of the "customers" is a regulatory agency concerned about the ultimate disposal of the products, then the potential cost of ignoring customer requirements can escalate even higher.

The early design process remains a grey area that is still mostly art and less science. The PC-Jr., like others that do not quite click, is an example of a product born of this grey zone (See Figure 5-1). Yet this grey area is absolutely critical to success, especially in a fast-moving product market. Get it wrong at the start and you put large amounts of money, time, and customer confidence at risk.

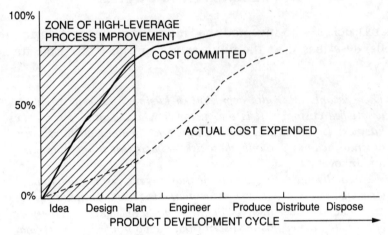

Figure 5-1 Design effort& product cost

Studies show that this grey area remains glaringly unattended by American firms. When asked what factors caused product development delays, an extensive study of electronic company CEOs concluded that excess time spent in the design stage, delays in identifying market needs, and last-minute design changes were the most prevalent contributors.[1] *An inability to understand that customer needs drive product development is an Achilles heel of contemporary Western management.* Paradoxical as it seems for the United States, the nation that invented Madison Avenue and its claims of fathoming the innermost depths of consumer opinion, numerous examples encountered by the author reveal a simple admission: "No one asked the customer."

In one case, a medical instruments company developed a technically superb monitoring device. But the engineer-designers failed to consider a vital user requirement: easy-to-manipulate dials and knobs. The oversight cost the company four months of redesign and production delays that allowed a competitor to capture market share. In a similar case, a manufacturer of a high-powered computer workstation turned out a whiz-bang machine. But it, too, had a "knob" problem. Every time a diskette was inserted into its slot, power would be shut off. The on-off switch had been placed so close to the slot that users' fingers inadvertently touched it.

A failure to understand the most basic customer needs can extract enormous penalties when a competitor is the one who gets the customer requirement right. This is the infamous Ampex lesson. Inventor of video recording equipment in 1956, the firm owned two-thirds of the market for the subsequent twenty years. RCA held the balance. Then in 1976, Sony first appeared in the same market. Ampex failed to gauge or respond to evolving customer needs for compact, high-quality, affordable units. It stayed on the high end, producing expensive equipment for professional-media users. Meanwhile VCR technology evolved, and the opportunity to tap a global mass market migrated rapidly and decisively offshore into Japanese hands.

TOO LATE...

Even GM's vaunted Saturn—designed with the customer in mind—took eight years to develop, thirty-six months over schedule. By the time it reached showrooms, it was a nice, cheap car but only just *another* car in a crowded field. What new benefit is delivered to a Saturn customer that is not already fully satisfied by other car makers? During the same period Honda or Toyota turned out not one, but two to three brand-new models each. Toyota, during a fourteen-month span in the Japanese market, introduced six brand-new cars, vans, and small trucks. In the United States, Toyota's 1991 Tercel sells for $100 less than the Saturn. Yet net profits on Toyota's American sales run four times higher than GM's profits. Even the come-from-nowhere upstart, Hyundai, a Korean company that did not even make cars when GM first conceived the Saturn project, managed to put several new models into the North American market.

NEXT IN LINE

A customer is traditionally viewed as the end user of a product or service, but there are many intermediaries, departments, suppliers, or distributors who add value to a product as it moves through different hands. In this more complex view, the customer is anyone "next in line."

This alters the concept and the perception of being "customer driven." It puts a different emphasis on all two-way value-adding interrelationships between specialized departments or functions inside a company as well as external partners: suppliers, distributors, and end users. Each is another's customer. Indeed, external links are acquiring more importance as reliance on outsourcing parts, research, or administrative services increases through supplier/partner networks and strategic alliances. Seen in these terms, customer relationships can be expressed as "do unto others as they would do unto you."

Dependencies are becoming strategically important to a degree that blurs the traditional definition of supplier. One example is the contracting of a company's internal information system management to large computer vendors such as IBM or DEC, or to systems houses such as EDS. This changes the idea of a supplier. From merely being the low-bid winner of a contract to meet fixed specifications, the supplier is actually an integral part of a team, sharing in the company's risks and rewards.

Visiting Ford's Rawsonville Plant in 1985, the author learned a minor but important lesson. Workers had just started an employee-involvement program instituted to improve sadly diminished quality standards. One team had decided to tackle a nagging problem. At one station on the assembly line, workers had to insert a small spring into a motor mechanism. Invariably the springs came jumbled together in a box, and it took time to disentangle them one by one. The newly established quality team sent a complaint letter to the vendor with the signatures of all its members: "Fix the mess or we will buy somewhere else." This direct complaint, a novel approach, got immediate results; a formal complaint might have been buried within a bureaucratic process. Springs soon came in boxes with dividers: one spring; one divider. The supplier may have been producing a fine spring as far as the end product was concerned, but it had just learned to reflect the practical concerns of the next person in line.

Depending on the product or the service, the actual customer is the next person in line. The next person in line is ultimately the end customer. Customer-driven quality is designed to meet customer requirements and to deliver the whole firm and its partners in meeting them.

This was not always understood by even the best in their business. One of the world's largest consumer products companies discovered this when it decided to think of distributors as a "customer." As much as it felt it had mastered end user needs—the kind you or I might have—it saw an opportunity in working much more closely with major discount chains in designing packaging, deliveries, and promotions. Applying disciplined customer analysis techniques learned in part from the Japanese (see **QFD** in Chapter 9), it identified dozens of distributor needs that had otherwise been overlooked or poorly interpreted. Once translated into terminology comprehensible to design and delivery experts, it was possible to make significant changes in package sizes, lot sizes for delivery, and promotional methods. The experiment, initiated late in the 1980s, proved enormously successful. During a two-year period at least $200 million of additional sales revenue was generated. This meant market share gains in major discount chains at the expense of competing companies.

There are numerous ways in which the "customer chain" principle can lead to unexpected rewards. For companies, such as pharmaceuticals or chemicals, that feel the pressure of governmental regulations, public agencies are generally viewed as adversaries. The Environmental Protection Agency and Food and Drug Administration are examples. Treating them as customers can completely alter the perception of these agencies' needs and of their unique constituencies. Viewed from this perspective, it is possible to arrive at solutions that accommodate both the "customer"—a regulatory agency—and the supplier—the company with products affected by strict regulations. As environmental crises accelerate in number and scale, this approach may alleviate adversarial tensions that would otherwise be relegated to the courtroom for lengthy adjudication.

CUSTOMER NEEDS ARE MORE COMPLEX

While such insights are leading to new and often different perceptions of who the customer really is, the techniques for understanding customer needs are changing fast. It used to be that a friendly salesman could work with a client and return to his home office with an order selected out of a catalogue and a price list. That may have meant "being close to the customer."

Times have changed. The customer, particularly in consumer products, has direct needs that are easily and clearly communicated. But there are also *latent* ones he or she is not aware of or cannot describe. No customer knew, for example, that he or she needed a Xerox machine, or a FAX, or a Walkman, or notebook computers. Many people know they need products that are "easy to use," but they cannot tell you what "easy" means. Further, the language a customer uses often has absolutely no meaning to an engineer. Thus, a person who wants a computer keyboard that is "easy to the touch of a finger," must have this requirement *translated* into terms that are understandable to an engineer or to a technical specialist who can then tailor a solution. This requires identifying measurable characteristics such as speed per second or light intensity that will satisfy the customer requirement.

By focusing with a passion on the customer, Japanese corporations changed the rules of competition. In 1990, television ads for Mazda cars appeared showing a test car driver wearing a helmet and strange goggles. These, it turned out, were instruments that recorded the driver's eye movement. Mazda was demonstrating its method of analyzing subtle human functions— such as eye movement—in order to design a customer-preferred car. This method allows Mazda to probe latent needs and satisfy them in ways that "delight the customer." How many times have we reached in the dark for the interior light switch while driving 60 miles an hour? When things are not where they should be, you know it right away. The Macintosh computer, on the other hand, pleases users because it is intuitive. Things work as one might guess they might by clicking the mouse on this or that. Reading the user manual is not always necessary. This delights because it makes it so easy to use the computer. But what also delights are the unexpected extras like Hypercard software. No one expected to get it when they bought a Macintosh.

MEETING CUSTOMER
NEEDS AND PRIORITIES

Product development teams do not have to get it right every time to win. Even the best effort to understand customers can lead to naught. The will to keep trying and the ability to learn from prior mistakes are what count.

Juki is one of the world's largest industrial sewing machine companies. Like many other Japanese firms, it practices all the basics of Total Quality Management. It learned the hard way what it means to be customer driven. Early in the 1980s, Juki decided to enter the home market for electronic sewing machines. Laboriously, it studied its potential market of housewives and arrived at a shopping list of their requirements for a sewing machine. The whole effort was successfully translated into a product. The new machine, an electronic marvel, could do anything and everything. But Juki was rudely jarred. The machine did not sell. The reason—they soon found out—was that no one wanted to pay for *all* the features. There were just too many of them for any one person to be able to use. Some were of little interest to many users.

Juki started over. This time it prioritized customer requirements and only targeted those most demanded. This lowered the cost of production because each machine was simpler to produce. The product became a best-seller and was quickly reiterated with carefully selected new features to match needs in various niche markets.

The lesson learned in this case was not to yield to the temptation to let the engineer's technology wish-list of options overwhelm the customer. This discipline *optimizes use of resources. It makes it easier to get to market fast. And it makes it easier to add features in future product improvements.*

COMMUNICATING NEEDS...

To design, develop, and deliver a product successfully, the whole team—companywide, including suppliers and customers—must communicate seamlessly in defining needs and ways of meeting them from the very inception of a planning and development cycle. This early and ongoing communication is at the heart of the new management style.

Ford learned the basics when it launched "Team Taurus" in 1980. One of the first steps it took was to study its potential customers for ideas. A long list of desired features and qualities resulted that influenced early design decisions. These were easily communicated within the team because all the traditional departmental barriers were broken down. Lew Veraldi, the project leader, made sure that his people did not need to be authorized to talk to someone in a parallel function such as manufacturing or engineering. They just did it even if, according to Veraldi, "there was a lot of table banging to make sure it happened."

In a book entitled *The Fifth Discipline*, Peter Senge uses the concept of "mental models" to describe the pervasiveness of beliefs in GM. One belief stands out: "Everyone connected with the system has no need for more than a fragmented, compartmentalized understanding of the business."[2] This approach is reminiscent of Norman Rockwell's magazine cover showing about twenty faces of individuals talking on the telephone. Each picks up a bit of gossip from the previous person, until the last one—who actually started the rumor—hears a completely different story. By the time the product gets to the customer, it has no connection to his or her needs.

Ford designed the Edsel this way. Generations of GM cars were designed this way. Engineers were delegated tasks. The results were pieced together into products that were force-fed to customers through aggressive advertising. While this worked for several decades, the rules of the game changed during the 1960s and 1970s as Japanese cars started to reflect actual customer desires in looks, driving qualities, and cost. Between 1980 and 1990, GM spent $70 billion automating its factory operations, but it did little to streamline its management practices or improve its market share. It kept on selling big, heavy, committee-designed, chrome-laden cars.

Describing a particular project, John Hertig of Kendall/McGaw Pharmaceuticals explains the dilemma of old management practice as follows: "Without a formal analysis of customer needs, it is very easy to forget to communicate important needs to the design staff.... In Kendall/McGaw, the product line manager in Marketing has always been the key focal point in the organization with respect to providing information regarding customer requirements. This has, however, presented difficulties.... In the preceding 9 months leading into the project, three different people were responsible for this function." For Hertig consistency in the analysis of customer needs and group consensus across functional boundaries were needed and could be achieved only by improving communications.[3]

THE NEW RULES

CUSTOMER NEEDS & EMPLOYEE MOTIVATION

Soon after its traumatic postdivestiture adjustments starting in 1984, AT&T found itself unprepared to compete in an open marketplace. What made it more difficult was that workers had very little motivation to change. Dogmatic requirements of supervisors and other managers put labor and management at loggerheads. Yet this was the very same company that legitimately claimed to have invented "quality management" in the 1930s by pioneering the use of statistical process control techniques developed by Walter Shewhart and his younger disciple W. Edwards Deming.

Concerned about motivating workers to accept "quality" as a mainstay of AT&T operations, a small group got to work in an Atlanta, Georgia, manufacturing plant. One question it probed was workers' reactions to the word "quality." And what the group members found surprised them. On the one hand, *quality was perceived as highly negative*. It was something you did to meet a standard. Not meeting it meant punishment, or worse, a feeling of failure. It was common in this plant for managers to punish poor performance by sending workers home for two or three days without pay.

"You know something," a worker said, "that just destroyed your confidence. You had to go home and tell your kids why you were sent home. To them you looked like a loser."

On the other hand, *people will push beyond normal limits if the goal is achievable and satisfying*. If this was so, the core group asked, how could the idea of quality be refocused to tap an enormous pool of latent energy in their work force? The answer was in the simple idea of meeting customer requirements. The more specific the requirements, the more workers felt motivated to meet them. And, of course, the inverse: The more remote the customer, the more the worker felt unattached or unmotivated (see Figure 5-2).

AT&T's Atlanta team graphed their conclusions in the form outlined above.[4] Surprisingly, the best quality was achieved, according to the graph, when both pride and meeting customer expectations were highest. It did not matter, in other words, that workers had a lot of pride in their work; if they were producing something that did not meet a customer expectation, quality suffered. AT&T's findings were surprising on another point, too.

Figure 5-2 Quality chart

"The theme, 'Do It Right the First Time' will backfire in America," company experts concluded. One reason is that to Americans "right the first time" connoted "perfection." AT&T's study revealed that "underlying 'perfection' was the notion of 'The End'— of no place left to go—death." A far more acceptable motivation to American workers was the link of quality with "it works for the customer."

Customer-driven management strategies are many-faceted. They affect motivations of workers as much as they affect market position and profitability. The core principle, however, rests in creating communication patterns that weave through all the value-adding boundaries. Hence, the relevance of cross-function teams.

RULE #2: Continuous improvement

Continuous improvement is what great chefs do when they translate personal recipes into cookbooks. They have to study each recipe, measure ingredients, record cooking times, and improve the recipes through continued experimentation. The chefs' experience and judgment must be turned into quantifiable data. To say "some of this" or "a little more" of that provides little useful guidance. A cookbook needs accurate instructions. The goal is not only to gain mastery over a process but to make it both *replicable and improvable*.

Continuous improvement is based on an ability of a whole workforce to generate and communicate **factual knowledge** *of its day-to-day operations. Problems and their origins are understandable only if the whole value chain is analyzed for causes and effects. The procedure is carried out again and again in reiterative cycles.* Thus, "management by facts" replaces guesswork and judgment.

Statistical process control (SPC) provides a mathematically sound technique for monitoring and improving performance. It takes out the guesswork by basing judgments, tests, and improvements on factual evidence. *SPC structures and standardizes the gathering and communication of information* so that a worker can make a distinction between one-of-a-kind problems (a defect caused by a freak accident) and systemic problems (a problem caused by a machine getting progressively worn down).

Statistically generated knowledge also provides feedback on how well *a whole system* performs and what its capabilities are. This not only streamlines day-to-day performance but assists in higher-level decisions. Strategy is an example. A corporation can better frame long-term opportunities if it has full knowledge of its day-to-day performance capabilities. Otherwise, the corporation is like the general with great plans but no idea of whether his troops can shoot straight or read a campaign map.

Measuring performance in cost or financial accounting terms is largely useless. Such data does not really tell you whether a customer's need is or is not met. Moreover, it is generally gathered after the fact, reaches the decision-makers two to three months after the conclusion of an activity, and may only satisfy Securities and Exchange Commission (SEC) requirements of quarterly performance reports.

This is what Analog Devices, a semiconductor and instruments company based in Massachusetts, discovered in 1988. Ray Stata, President and Founder of the $450 million firm, was concerned that sales were not increasing rapidly enough. Curious about what might be wrong, he and his VP of Quality, Art Schneiderman, queried supervisory staff. Each was asked the same probing question: "If the phone rang right now and it was a customer calling, what would they say?" To their surprise the answer was almost uniformly the same: "The order is late."

This led Stata and Schneiderman to a difficult conclusion. *"Our management tools just were not telling us what we needed to know about our operations."* Quarterly executive council decisions at Analog Devices were based on reporting data on twenty different variables, all of them financial in character. "We realized that this was at the core of our problem," said Schneiderman. Two years later things took a significant turn. Quarterly council meetings still looked at eighteen variables, but only five were a dollars-and-cents numbers. The rest focused on quality, for example, how well customer needs were being met. Top on the list was data on delivery times.

The new data allowed managers to focus on day-to-day improvements and communicate them companywide. The new tracking system allowed each employee at Analog Devices to feel the impact of his or her efforts on something that had direct and immediate meaning: customer satisfaction. This meant a great deal more than reading about earnings ratios or cost to budget ratios. Strategy and operations were aligned. By targeting them with real data on performance, improvement efforts were prioritized and focused.

One of Analog's innovations was the discovery that constant improvement has a "half-life" characteristic. In other words, a defect rate can be reduced by 50 percent in a logical beginning-to-end cycles of activity, and 50 percent again, and again in cycles all with similar time periods. The formula they devised (see Figure 5-3) was simple:[5] With this new metric of improvement in hand, they used the PDCA cycle as a method of planning the process necessary to achieve each targeted half-life improvement. The improvements reported by the company's semiconductor division using these methods are impressive: Some of these numbers indicate improvements of 50

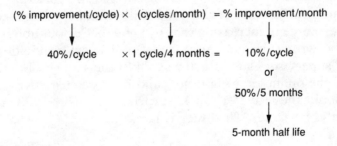

(% improvement/cycle) × (cycles/month) = % improvement/month

40%/cycle   × 1 cycle/4 months =   10%/cycle

or

50%/5 months

5-month half life

Figure 5-3

to 500 times! It is a persuasive substantiation of the figurative 30 percent factor that I introduced in the opening chapters. Tackling it with TQM methods can be enormously productive. Process quality metrics of the sort developed by Analog Devices are now part of the quarterly review process by the executive council.

METRIC	1987	1990	1992 est.
External			
On Time delivery	85%	96%	99.8%
Outgoing defect level	500ppm	230ppm	10ppm
Lead Time	10 wks	5.4 wks	3 wks
Internal			
Manufacturing cycle time	15 wks	8 wks	4–5 wks
Process defect level	5000ppm	1100ppm	10ppm
Yield	20%	38%	50%
Time to market	36 mos	n.a.	6 mos

Source: Analog Devices (Norwood, MA)

HOLISTIC MANAGEMENT

The successful chef must orchestrate numerous activities for a meal to be successful. Table settings, seating, menus, waiters, sous-chef, vegetable, meat, fish, bread, and other supplies need to be on hand. To succeed, the chef must understand the intimate interrelationship of all the elements that go into making a meal a memorable experience. This is, in effect, what Deming and his quality management peers, the likes of Joseph Juran and A. V. Feigenbaum, understood. No worker could improve a procedure he or she was involved in without *also comprehending the whole process*. It makes no sense for a worker to detect a problem at his or her moment of performing a task without being able to correct the source of the problem, which might originate several stages earlier in the customer chain. Continuous improvement has to be holistic in order to detect and correct problems. Put differently, it is not enough to simply see the task at hand.

THE SEAMLESS ENTERPRISE

Studying this issue, David Garvin, a professor at the Harvard Business School, compared attitudes of supervisory level workers in Japanese and American air conditioner firms. "Japanese supervisors appear to view the production process in its entirety; both the design and maintenance of equipment are considered part of production, even though they involve different kinds of activities." He concluded that "among U.S. supervisors, the focus appears to be on tasks and activities."[6]

Which one would you buy?
Quality Performance and Ratings for Air Conditioners (median)
(9 U.S. companies; 7 Japanese companies)

	Internal Failures*	External Failures**	Number of Plants
Japanese companies:			
All	0.95	0.6	7
U.S. plants:			
Best	9.00	7.2	2
Better	26.00	10.5	3
Fair	63.50	9.8	3
Poor	135.00	22.9	3

*Assembly line defects per 100 units
**Service calls per 100 units under first-year warranty

Garvin's study established an important correlation between holistic attitudes and high-quality results in a production environment. The defect and service call data of U.S. manufacturers is dramatically higher. Today Japanese air conditioner manufacturers are making dramatic inroads into a U.S. market segment that was traditionally considered immune from foreign competitors.

Strip away the fat in a serialized process and you will end up with many tasks and activities that can be scheduled to occur simultaneously. Go back for a moment to our restaurant chef.

RULE #3: Concurrency

THE NEW RULES

When an order comes in, the chef does not cook the meat first, then the sauce, then the vegetables, and then heat a plate to put it on. This would be a disaster. It would taste awful, take too long, and less people could be served. Downstream needs are taken into account at the start.

A good chef produces a meal concurrently. All wasted effort and time is stripped away. All of the elements are planned to culminate in the best possible dish in the shortest possible time. This sort of concurrency is really a description of a horizontal management process that forces connections across the organization and its suppliers and customers. Downstream needs are taken into account at the start.

In the world of complex technological products, the purpose of concurrent engineering is to resolve problems that "are the result of a proliferation of functional specialties within government and industry," states the Institute for Defense Analyses. "These specialists tend to form communities that are called 'stovepipes.' Communication tends to be confined to the different communities.... Horizontal communication is less effective when the influence of 'stovepipes' is strong. Because horizontal communication is essential for concurrent engineering, any initiative that tends to create a new 'concurrent engineering' specialty will be a fundamental contradiction of its goals."

Much like the chef at work, or even like parallel processing in a computer, concurrency allows varied tasks to be initiated simultaneously to improve designs, shorten development cycles, and make more effective use of limited resources (money and people's time). Concurrency works only if accompanied by fluid horizontal communication between key players on a team.

Concurrency is a reaction to the "Send it over the transom" design ethic. The non-value-adding administrative inefficiencies in managing sequential or serialized hand-offs, whether it is aircraft, financial services, cars, hotels, or software, eat up enormous financial and time resources. The reason is that a hand-off—no matter how well the prior team completes its task—is still a hand-off. It generally excludes direct one-on-one communication that would otherwise catch problems before the next person—the next customer in line—sees the work. Since the latter have not had a voice in influencing or reviewing the prior task, what is passed on often needs to be reworked to meet downstream requirements.

This process can be highly contentious. The "upstream" people are prone to blame the "downstream" ones for messing things up and vice versa. The walls between chimneys only get thicker as each side tries to insulate itself from blame. And because reward systems mirror the chimneys, the pressure on each chimney is even greater to blame someone else if things do not go right.

CONCURRENCY IS MORE THAN MEETING DEADLINES

Concurrency can significantly shorten the time required to complete projects. Participants in a project managed this way communicate horizontally from the very beginning. It makes no sense for tasks to be managed in parallel if no one is talking together or consulting one another. That would only compound errors and flaws when it came time to cementing all the separate tasks together. This is why traditional planning tools that depend solely on time or cost measures to manage tasks (such tools as Project Evaluation and Review Techniques [PERT] and Critical Path Method [CPM] or GANTT scheduling charts) have limited use. They work when it comes to planning quantifiable tasks like gadgets being milled on a machine. But they do little to account for subjective human interactions, particularly those that occur between horizontal tasks. PERT and GANTT tools and multitudes of software programs that support them are not designed to graphically show "horizontal" or "concurrent" links such as design review meetings or informal but vital information exchange meetings. Those, it turns out, are the heart of what makes concurrency work.

SUMMARY

These new rules of the game—customer-driven products, continuous improvements, and concurrency—are forcing a new management style upon us. Central to it is the teaming of managers and workers laterally across their companies. To do this, more and more firms are turning to the TQM model and the cross-function process characteristic of it as a benchmark for making improvements and for stimulating their own innovative solutions. However, understanding the essentials of the TQM process is a first step in adapting to the new rules.

Notes

Chapter 5

1. Report by Ernst & Young, New York, 1991.

2. Peter Senge, *The Fifth Discipline*, Doubleday, New York, 1990, p. 176.

3. John Hertig, presentation to Goal/QPC Sixth Annual Conference, Boston, December 1989.

4. Lewis J. Hatala and Marilyn R. Zuckerman, "What Moves Americans to Achieve the Impossible in Your Company," Presentation to the National Conference on Productivity and Quality, Washington, D.C., April 1991.

5. Art Schneiderman, "Total Quality Management," Analog Devices, Inc., Unpublished Presentation Materials.

6. David A. Garvin, "Quality Problems, Policies, and Attitudes in the United States and Japan: An Exploratory Study," *Academy of Management Journal*, Vol. 29, No. 4, 1986.

6: THE TQM ELEMENTS

Total quality management and cross functions are intertwined. One cannot be achieved without the other. Unlike conventional management that focuses more single-mindedly on getting vertical functions to produce "results," the focus of the TQM and cross-function control is "process" management. This achieves unified and more effective companywide results by managing process laterally across the company's chimneys. Analog Devices' "half-life" achievements are an example.

The basic elements of TQM are vision, strategy, policy deployment, daily management results, and targeted cross functions managed by companywide teams (see Figure 6-1). Except for the last, the elements will be familiar to many who have studied or applied quality methods.

THE TQM ELEMENTS

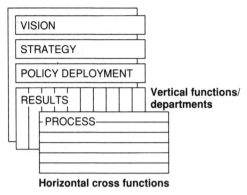

Figure 6-1 The Basic Elements of TQM

VISION

A vision is an over-the-horizon expression of corporate purpose. It can be merely a slogan handed down for others to parrot. Or, better, it can be a set of deeply felt values that are collectively arrived at through debate, discussion, and consensus. Vision-setting starts at the top with corporate leaders expressing long-term direction. Drucker's marketing concept is a strong platform upon which to build a TQM corporate vision. One reason is that it commits a firm to deliver its full energies to serve its customer.

Here's an example of simple, straightforward statement reflecting these principles:

> *Total quality is a commitment by all employees at all levels to maximize consumer/customer satisfaction through innovation and continual improvement in the quality and value of all products and services.*[1]

In contrast, many corporate vision statements refer first to shareholder values, and last (if at all) to customers or employees. The latter is reminiscent of President Nohmura and his tent company described in the foreword. He remembered once taking pride in selling defective products because it seemed an easy way to make a profit. That changed when his company was humiliated and almost bankrupted by the collapse of a huge inflated tent at a fair. Nohmura changed his vision that day and has since strengthened his enterprise in his customers eyes. The result, the by-product of his vision, is an even more profitable company.

Crafting a vision can be catalytic, particularly if it leads to a stronger sense of "cross-functional" unity and purpose. A vision carries a powerful competitive punch if it coalesces the energies of a whole enterprise. An example of this happened when 300 of AT&T's most senior Network Operating Group (NOG) managers met at a hotel for a three-day no-holds-barred meeting late in 1988. What surfaced was a deep distrust of the group's leaders. These executives were calling for a new behavior by sending out memos "empowering" subordinates to act in the company's best interest. Yet the very same executives were announcing large-scale layoffs. No one knew why they should bother being empowered if they were going to be out of a job.

Three days of discussion ultimately led to a spirited commitment to a "new" NOG in which managers were *truly empowered to take risks in behalf of their customers*. To most in the room this was the first time a slogan had been turned into an operational *vision* they could both believe in and professionally act on.

Once a vision is crafted, the next task is to translate it into a coherent set of strategies. In the TQM model, aligning the whole company through cross-function teams ensures uniform adherence to the vision, strategies, and policies.

STRATEGY

The determination of *how* a company can best operate is as important as knowing *what* it will achieve in terms of products, technologies, or purely financial business goals. Thus, an effective corporate strategy must describe both clear objectives and the means for achieving them. These reflect the judgment and knowledge of those who will execute it as well as their ability to work as a cohesive team in so doing. This puts cross-function knowledge teams into the limelight as a primary mechanism for managing the processes needed to meet the strategic objective.

"Results and Process" as the Strategy

Take the example of product strategy. Depending on the type of product and the point its has reached on a life-cycle "S" curve, the strategy can be *revolutionary*, for example, introducing products or technologies never seen before (such as the first Xerox copier), *evolutionary*, for example, improving on an existing idea (such as a copier with faster features), or *customized*, for example, reconfiguring an existing product to meet one-of-a-kind requirements. But just to know WHAT the product strategy is going to be is not enough. HOW it will be achieved is equally important. Aiming for a revolutionary product suggests a very different set of organizational capabilities than aiming for a customized product.

This three-tiered product classification can be further refined into subcategories of product types each of which, if implemented, requires different cross-departmental teaming methods. Two academics, Don Clausing of MIT and Stuart Pugh of the University of Strathclyde in Scotland, offer an interesting breakdown of product-strategy refinements. Each can be used to fine-tune cross-function process strategies and methods.

PRODUCT TYPES IN THE CLAUSING/PUGH MATRIX

Presentation by Prof. Don Clausing at Vanderbilt University (May 1991)

PRODUCT	EXAMPLE
Genesis	First of a kind (breakthrough)
Revolutionary	Xerox 914 in 1960
New to a firm	Kodak Copier
Clean sheet	Generational change: Xeroc 1075 in 1981 (a third-generation product)
Market niche	Xerox 2400 (mid-volume)
Market niche	Generational change
Associated	A product linked to another such as a laser printer based on Xerox technology
Variants	Small changes: the Xerox 1090 (faster)
Customized	—

It is incumbent on the strategists to take into account the whole firm's process abilities to deliver results. In this manner, strategy reflects a marriage of cross-function process capabilities and specific product goals. It would be foolish, in other words, for a company to chase after a revolutionary product if it did not have internal know-how and resources—or the capability of allying with external players who could achieve a breakthrough. An effective marriage of HOW and WHAT is not possible in conventionally managed firms that do not have cross-function process management control methods in place.

In addition, products can be conceived as total systems or as combinations of subcomponents and piece parts. A strategy might concentrate on systems-level changes or simply on components. Clausing and Pugh also address this issue. They devise a "Commonality Matrix" consisting on the horizontal axis of sources of ideas such as current products and competitive products, analogous ones, or ones made up of totally new technologies, and consisting on the vertical axis of the levels of products such as system, subsystem, or piece parts (see Figure 6-2). This breakdown offers the strategist an even finer grain of choices to optimize the firm's cross-departmental capabilities. At one extreme of the commonality matrix are *dynamic products* or what Clausing and Pugh describe as "new" systems, components

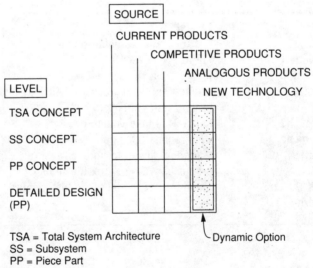

Figure 6-2   Commonality Matrix

or piece parts consisting of all new technology. At the other are *static* products with no new technology built into it. A dynamic product strategy (shaded area) would consist of all new technologies in the four boxes in the right-hand column. Static would mean reused ideas on all the left-hand columns. "The ultimate in commonality," says Clausing, "is that the piece part design is the same, for example, the same part used in more than one product. However, if all parts are the same, then two products are the same; not very interesting."

An example of companies reaching for dynamic solutions at the component level is illustrated by a competitive race in small computers with powerful microprocessors. Compaq, Dell, and AST are major players aggressively offering their customer plug–in upgrades of key new components such as faster microprocessors and other key operating features.

By using a hierarchical breakdown (system, subsystem, component, piece part) of product development choices such as Clausing and Pugh propose, a firm can then better align a product strategy to the capabilities of the firm. This puts "process" alongside "product" as a component of a firm's competitive strategy. The combination is a major distinguishing factor between "old" management and "new" TQM.

When Process Alone Is the Strategy

Process itself can be the strategy if the product remains *static* but process-driven improvements in its quality, cost, or delivery are targeted for improvement. This adds a third axis of process-driven choices to the Commonality Matrix and thereby increases the range of strategic options for a firm. This works, however, only if there is a high level of lateral process communication and co-ordination across all parts of the corporation and its supplier and partner links.

A hypothetical product strategy for a new car 'ENGINE 'X' may, for example, concentrate on a *dynamic* solution at a sub-system level, for example, a new turbine blade design in a turbocharger, but with "cost" as the process-driven differentiator for the total engine assembly. The optimal "process" tactics necessary to achieve a low-cost advantage would be the responsibility of a cross-function team. It is in this sense that the WHAT and the HOW are linked to strategy in the TQM model.

THE SEAMLESS ENTERPRISE

POLICY DEPLOYMENT

Policy is the translation of strategy into executable actions. *Management by Policy* is substantially different from the commonly applied practice of Management by Objective (MBO). MBO is sometimes characterized as "Management by Asking for the Most and Giving the Least." Because it is a negotiation between the superior and the person next in rank, the first wants to get the most out of the next one below, and the latter wants to do the least. The result is a set of compromises that reflect negotiating skills of decision makers in various divisions or departments. This rarely takes the whole enterprise into account since the negotiation is carried out solely within chimney boundaries and rules. Eventually it leads to suboptimal companywide performance because policy decisions are made in fragmented parts and not as components of a whole.

"MANAGEMENT BY POLICY"

When I joined Sylvania in the 1950s, it was a relatively small company. The individuals who started it were still in charge. They lived in the community. They knew everybody and really took that as part of their job. Then things changed. For example, I remember when management by objective, what is known as MBO, came in as a new program with a lot of fanfare. There was a form you had to fill out with a lot of numbers. The reaction was "What the hell are they doing? I always did this, but now they want me to fill out a form."

Rather than an organic thing it became a numbers game. You had to quantify your objectives then submit a report. It quickly became an enshrined ritual. The price of it was that individual commitment was replaced by compliance with a specified and standardized format. Without the direct human commitment it didn't take long for performance to deteriorate.

Kemp Dwenger, then export manager for electronic products at Sylvania; later vice-president for International Sales at GTE

Management by Policy—also known as Policy Deployment or Hoshin Kanri—is quite different. Rather than negotiating policy agreement, one at a time, corporate policy is a top-down directive. There is considerable effort spent, however, to coordinate the execution [or deployment] of the policy across all

THE TQM ELEMENTS

departments so that the efforts of one do not impede the next. This optmizes companywide results. Jim Watson, vice president of Worldwide Quality for Texas Instruments Semiconductor Group, explains Policy Deployment as a "process for identifying a small number of key actions that will produce 'Breakthrough.' The objective is the condition desired after Breakthrough...." He adds, "To set organizational objectives that support top management goals for the business and which put the customer first at each level requires a top-down and bottom-up cycle of communication, negotiation, and alignment."[2]

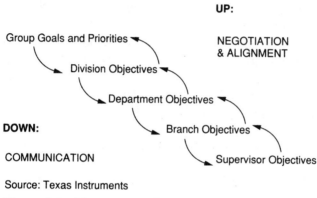

Source: Texas Instruments

Figure 6-3 Management by Policy

This is carried out in a reiterative flow through quarterly reviews and annual diagnostic audits (see Figure 6-3). Policy deployment is directed downward. Feedback loops back upward. It is not the job of those below to argue the policy but to determine how they will best achieve it. The feedback loops allow senior managers to balance the "HOWs" of those below. Subordinates are given substantial latitude in HOW they execute the directive.

This is quite different from the common American belief that good managers are "tough" managers who both dictate policies and rigorously enforce them. "Good" managers, in the traditional view, focus single-mindedly on results. When they order those below to cut costs by slashing every departmental budget by 10 percent across the board, everybody is expected to fall into line. There is no process management leading to a fundamental improvement, only an order. Never mind that something of importance to a customer is axed or that the impact of one department's arbitrary 10 percent cut may negatively affect another department. This widespread style of management is leaves no latitude for the subordinate to establish an *improved process* that might yield a 10 percent or greater cost reduction by some means other than an arbitrary request to cut 10 percent off a budget. And it provides absolutely no mechanism for coordinating the execution of policy between departments.

Policy deployment, on the other hand, brings *companywide consistency* to top-level directives. An annual policy directive may address a critical market requirement, such as a safer car. The policy might be to improve safety by a factor of two. Quantified targets are then formulated. In the case of Texas Instruments, for example, the company focus was on improving business processes in order to gain a competitive advantage with customers. Six business processes in control and finance were analyzed and rated. By the company's own measuring system any rating below seven makes it a candidate for what it calls a "breakthrough":

ITEM	PERFORMANCE RATING
Forecast	3
Update	7
Accounts Receivable	8
Close	2
Accounts Payable	7
Asset Inventory	8

As a policy directive cascades down, every department and section will have an impact by defining its own plan for meeting the goals. By focusing companywide effort on a single policy directive (such as "Forecasting," which had a three), the results are cumulative and dramatic instead of being dispersed and diffuse. In each case checkpoints are established for gauging progress and taking measures to change or improve the process. "The hardest thing for us," says TI's Jim Watson, "has been to shift our attention to process and away from pure results. It is difficult to break old habits."

THE TQM ELEMENTS

RESULTS: DAILY MANAGEMENT BASICS

Statistical process control (SPC) is the aspect of total quality practices most written about and best understood in the United States. The purpose of SPC is to put basic and easy-to-understand analytical tools into the hands of workers. SPC is a bottom-up process of managing daily tasks: information flows from the smallest unit of production, the single work station, up into the organization.

Any continuous process can be monitored to determine whether it is under control or going out of control. If it is out of control, corrections can be made before a process crashes and causes far greater cost in lost time and effort. The vaunted "quality circle" was invented to empower workers to analyze and deliberate about statistical process data and the ways in which problems they encountered could be corrected. Because corrections usually involve activities that happen upstream, workers must be cognizant of the whole process. In this environment, the manager's role turns into that of a coach rather than an adversary. This is a dramatic departure from Tayloristic ideas that put the onus for determining work tasks on the manager. "The work of every workman is fully planned out by the management at least one day in advance," wrote Frederick Winslow Taylor, "and each man receives in most cases complete written instructions, describing in detail the task which he is to accomplish, as well as the means to be used in doing the work."[3]

Bottom-up quality is rich in principles, tools, and techniques. The Seven Old Tools and the Seven New (see Figure 6-4) perfected and widely applied in Japan, are now recognized in the United States as vital to management. Many of these reflect Deming's 14 quality principles for managers. Other experts such as Juran, Feigenbaum, and Crosby have their own equally compelling lists of dos and don'ts. All can be applied to almost any aspect of a corporation's day-to-day activities, from sales, to manufacturing, to engineering design, to distribution. Managing by facts, continuous improvement, and worker empowerment are common features of the quality basics. Other tools and techniques include just-in-time (JIT), or productive maintenance (PM); Taguchi Methods, which help the designer anticipate the downstream effects of engineering decisions; quality function deployment (QFD), which help teams collaborate in

THE SEAMLESS ENTERPRISE

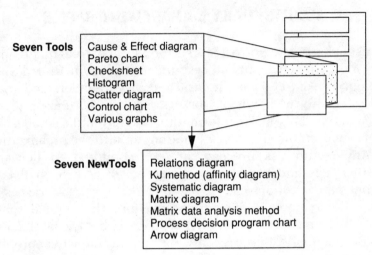

Figure 6-4 The Seven Old Tools and the Seven New Tools

defining customer requirements and the best methods of respond-ing to them.

All these quality tools share one significant feature: they are fact-based tools. The purpose of the tool is to generate and record facts in ways that are not just of immediate managerial value but that create a common companywide "language." This allows *continuous improvements* to be understood and executed uniformly across organizational boundaries.

The basic quality tools are sometimes referred to as "daily management tools." Their utility is in monitoring real-time per-formance and diagnosing problems at the root. The invention of cause-and-effect "fishbone" diagrams illustrates this systemic approach by interweaving people, materials, methods, and ma-chines into a single process flow.

The catalogue of quality tools and an ability to use them are preconditions to installing a system of cross-function manage-ment. Without them, the manager is left powerless to meaning-fully measure or control day-to-day tasks and activities.

BUILDING THE TQM MODEL

Cross-function management is an integral part of these basic TQM elements. CFM's power is in reorienting the communication and information flows laterally across the company into more effective value–adding activities. This overcomes a fundamental flaw of the vertically managed results–focused firm. As explained by David Hanna, a manager from Procter & Gamble, "How much you produced today is treated as independent of whether it has an impact on any other activity." This approach, sometimes called Machine Theory, "stem[s] from the assumption that an organization is like a machine: a collection of parts that need to be standardized and centrally controlled."[4] The challenge, therefore, is to bridge quality across the whole enterprise. One place to start is with a more holistic management model. The first major linkage is between directives driven from the top down and performance capabilities driving information upward uniformly from all departments (see Figure 6-5). Having reached this point, the firm still faces a more daunting challenge: the horizontal integration of all the vertical activities

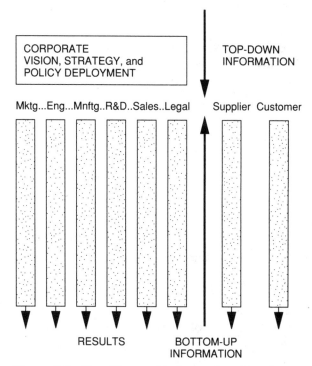

Figure 6-5   Two Flows of Information: Top-down directives and bottom-up performance capability

82

THE SEAMLESS ENTERPRISE

so that non-value-adding barriers, such as administrative procedures or different dysfunctional reward systems, are eliminated. Cross-function methods of teaming are used to induce lateral communication and to establish uniform performance standards companywide. Through horizontal interdepartmental collaboration, the fulfilment of corporate objectives can be made far more effective (see Figure 6-6).

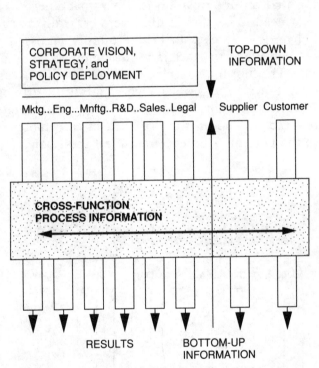

Figure 6-6 Horizontal flow of process information

By establishing strong lateral communications, cross-function management addresses problems that cannot be effectively solved by any one vertical division or department or simply by issuing top-down executive orders. Meeting of customer expectations through quality or warranty management is an example. Clearly, no single department is solely responsible, and certainly no single department is a "quality or warranty assurance department." Only by coordinating all pertinent departments can a "warranty" control or "customer satisfaction" process be established that cuts across all functions.

When Toyota first set out to tackle the warranty-control process in the 1960s, it identified three principal activities: (1) improvement of the quality of the total process from product planning, to product design, to production planning, to mass production, to purchasing, sales, and service; (2) creation of activities that would guarantee quality at key inspection moments; and (3) creation of activities and standards that ensure that (1) and (2) above are correctly implemented.

By focusing on "warranty" as a companywide concern, Toyota was able to map out a comprehensive "product-development process." It ensured maximum customer satisfaction by minimizing warranty costs to the company. This was achieved by broadening cross-function procedures and responsibilities across departments, supplier, and distributor boundaries. These practices propagated widely not just within Toyota and Komatsu, both early innovators, but throughout corporate Japan. In 1986, a study of 82 Deming prize–winning companies established a ranking of issues managed by cross function:

CROSS FUNCTIONS	#OF COMPANIES
Quality/Warranty	59
Cost	54
Quantity/Delivery	39
New product development	22
Sales/Ordering	14
Personnel/Training	11
Safety/Environment	7
Purchasing	6
Information	3

Cross-function teams such as those listed above are empowered by a CEO to develop and improve "horizontal management processes." The novel role of these teams becomes evident. It introduces a third direction of information flow to the web of communication. This is why it is central to the success of Total Quality Management practices.

Notes

Chapter 6

1. Vision statement from Nippon Zeon (1985) as presented by Larry Huston (Procter & Gamble).

2. James Watson (Texas Instruments), paper presented to the Dartmouth Conference on Cross-Functional Management (Thayer School of Engineering), Hanover, New Hampshire, March 1989.

3. Frederick Winslow Taylor, *Scientific Management*, Harper & Brothers Publishers, New York, 1947, p. 39.

4. David P. Hanna, *Designing Organizations for High Performance*, Addison Wesley, Reading, Massachusetts, 1988, p. 4.

7: KNOWLEDGE TEAMS

An increasing number of knowledge workers will have a "functional" home but do their work in a team with other knowledge workers from other functions and disciplines. The more advanced the knowledge worker's knowledge the more likely it is that he will do his work and make his contribution in cross–functional teams rather than in his own functional component.[1] Peter F. Drucker

The new rules call for a new style of management behavior. Seamless in the way they process information, cross-function teams are a central operational feature. They serve as company *process* "knowledge teams" with a collective understanding of a subject (see Figure 7-1). This serves to interweave the activitites of vertical silos in specialized functions such as "manufacturing engineering," whose goal is to produce measurable results such as production units off an assembly line, or designs in an engineering center.

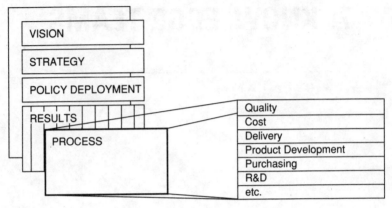

Figure 7-1 Cross-function "knowledge teams"

THE MAKING OF "KNOWLEDGE TEAMS"

A cross-functional team is empowered to treat a process in its totality, and not within narrow departmental jurisdictions. The process may be *quality assurance* (how you meet customer requirements), managing *cost* reductions, or managing *delivery* of product in quantities and times desired by a customer. Or the team may focus on an internally important process such a *safety and training, research and development, management information systems*, or *purchasing*. A team may also work to improve a *product-development* process. In each case, the group is the knowledgeable entity, not a specialized unit within.

The members of these knowledge teams represent a gamut of departments and external partners. Their goal is to optimize interdepartmental communication: Who needs to share what information with whom in order to achieve a desired outcome? Because the team members are line people, they represent their own self-interest by planning companywide processes that will help them in their own day-to-day business operations. Participation is seen as a win-win for everyone, the company included.

The members of a companywide process team work best if constituted from all line operations, divisions, or departments. The line members are not chosen because of their expertise in the horizontal function. When necessary, a specialist in the subject area may also be a member.

KNOWLEDGE TEAMS

There is no formal analog to such cross-function teams in American firms. Even though cross-function teams have existed on an ad hoc basis and cross-functional management has been broadly discussed by academics for many years, managing as a companywide process is still a black art. It is done when the need arises, more by guesswork than as a continuous disciplined activity. Companywide task forces or crisis management teams come and go on a case-by-case basis. There are few American precedents of companywide teams created to develop and improve generic processes.

This helps explain why product-development processes, for example, are too slow, too costly, and not always able to meet quality requirements. One team may get it right, another may not. There is no consistent method of conceiving and improving a product-development process.

A confidential academic report circulated about a blue-chip company's operations concluded the "manufacturing engineers and shop floor managers can [only] guess at the value of improvements in cycle time, quality or reductions of inventory. The incentive structure and the information system work together in a self-reinforcing structure to perpetuate the lack of information. Since information has historically not been gathered about factors such as inventory level and cycle time neither engineers nor shop floor managers are rewarded for reductions in their level: since neither engineers nor shop floor managers are rewarded for reductions in their level no information is gathered about them."[2] No one was knowledgeable about the whole process. In such circumstances valuable information slips between the cracks when decisions are made.

A mature, seamless corporation might count five to ten key cross-function teams, each one responsible for the "management process" of a specific horizontal activity. In time, each acquires operational knowledge that is strategically valuable to the firm: where the strengths and weaknesses are, how things get done, and how procedures can be improved. Together these company-wide knowledge teams constitute the eyes and ears of the whole system's capability. They embody a new form of corporate intelligence that cuts across departmental boundaries. As Professor Shigeru Mizuno notes: *"Since total quality activities are aimed at merging company-wide intellectual power.... all the information contained in the group [must] become the possession of the entire group...* This, in turn, leads to the generation of new ideas."

ELECTRONIC COMMUNICATION

If Professor Mizuno's vision is taken to encompass information flows among a corporation's global activitites, the sheer volume— not to speak of accessibility—of information to be transmitted presents new challenges to the telecommunications industry. Vastly extended data communication is a concept being promoted by Robert Kahn, an ex-offical of the Defense Advance Research Projects Agency (DARPA), as the basis for a new generation of "electronic highways" that will transport information nationwide much as conventional highways allow people and goods to be shipped. If implemented, it would become the backbone to extend virtual proximity or more extensive collaboratory opportunities to a far wider audience of users.

THE FUTURE IS NOW:

Searching vast computer data bases can be easier than consulting a card catalogue.... Users with little computer skills will soon be able to search through several terabytes of information or several trillion characters of text, in seconds. The Library of Congress, with 80 million items, contains an estimated 25 terabytes of information.

Already, an experimental computer library has linked 150 universities to 40 sources of information ranging from the National Institutes of Health data to corporate documents, and Shakespeare's plays...In 1989, Thinking Machines enlisted the support of Dow Jones, Apple Computer Inc. and the KPMG Peat Marwick accounting and consulting firm to design the computer library, called Wide Area Information Servers, or WAIS....

At Thinking Machines, the WAIS system serves as a "corporate memory," allowing employees to retrieve memos, documents and other internal information. Employees who may not be working together can share expertise.

"For the PC User Vast Libraries," *The New York Times,* 7/3/91

There are, of course, huge hurdles to overcome in meeting the ideal of full enterprisewide collaboratories. Large companies, because they are vertically organized, often have computer systems that mirror their top-down structures. Engineering departments might have HP, DEC, and Sun equipment. Accounting, personnel, and finance departments have IBM. One department's computers are not necessarily compatible with another's, and linking them together is far from trivial, politically as well as technologically. In many cases the major impediment to integrating computer systems is turf wars between senior managers who feel threatened by the loss of control over budgets, information, or subordinates. Oftentimes the *major* impediment is the group one would think most likely to argue the integration case: MIS (Management of Information Systems) departments. Because they have been organized as chimneys with authority to dictate computer solutions downward into complex organizations, they are often threatened by solutions that look "decentralized" or that do not conform to centralized management requirements. Another hurdle stands in the path of networked computer technology aimed at "integrating enterprises": the gap between what the tools themselves can do, for example, move bits of data in great volume between any two points, and the management style necessary to make effective use of the technology and the information it can make available. Enterprise integration, as a computer-driven concept, cannot work without a management style conducive to companywide teaming. Thus the growing importance of cross-functional management as an operational model of companywide group intelligence.

THE CATALYST: SYNTHESIS

The rising complexity of products, research alliances, joint ventures, supplier relationships, and globally distributed operations is putting a new cast on the character and composition of company teams. Not only do all these factors make communication more difficult, but the mechanics for getting things done is itself more complex. All this is causing new interest in the teaming process. How can one better manage, lead, reward, and guide companywide groups? How does one make such disparate and dispersed teams seamless in their day-to-day operations?

The need to "synthesize" is the catalyst forcing the rapid evolution of horizontal knowledge teams. As sources of information proliferate, as products and services get more complex, and as companies reach into global markets, marketplace survival is largely dependent on how well a firm, and subgroups within it, manages to add value to an enterprise's activity. This complexity makes it increasingly difficult for the individual person or department to be the sole depository of valuable knowledge, such as the master craftsmen of bygone days, or the brilliant engineer who could singlehandedly mastermind a product in more recent times.

When you "synthesize," says Dr. Russell Ackoff, a professor from the Wharton School of Finance and Economics, "you don't look at the thing to be explained as a whole to be taken apart, but as a part of a larger whole. You then attempt to explain the whole of which *it* is a part, and then extract an explanation of the thing you started with from an explanation of the whole." He terms this approach as "up and down again as opposed to down and up again." This is fundamental to the approach a knowledge team takes in treating companywide issues. As Dr. Ackoff points out, this process is counterintuitive. A cross-function team takes an issue such as high warranty costs and understands it as part of the whole before deciding how best to resolve it.

"If you take a system and take it apart to identify its components, and then operate those components in such a way that every component behaves as well as it possibly can [Author's note: This is the Tayloristic legacy embodied in scientific management], there is one thing of which you can be sure," says Ackoff. "The system as a whole will not behave as well as *it* can."[3]

The intriguing corollary is that "if a system is behaving as well as it can, none of its parts will be." If correct, this view could have a profound effect on how a corporation is managed. It means that to optimize companywide interests, each of its departments should not operate as efficiently as each might independently be capable of doing. The implication is no different than the sports analogy used in an earlier chapter. A basketball team made up of five solo super stars will not perform as well as simply good players who work exceedingly well as a team. They have a system, the solo starts do not (as is often evident in All-Star games).

The horizontal knowledge team's assignment is to describe the best process for managing a cross function. Its job is to balance the interrelationship of the parts so that the whole is the winner. In this sense the knowledge team is an organizational response to the three basic rules of TQM: customer-driven quality, continuous improvement, and concurrency. Customer needs cannot be properly served by specialized departments operating at arm's length of one another, with poor communication, difficult coordination, frustrating hand-offs ("That's not my department"), and inadequate sharing of information. Given the choice, customers will recognize the value of one-stop customer service, particularly with more complex products or services. They want a single "system" responding to them not a patchwork of "parts."

Effectiveness is a social concept: it applies to groups. Efficiency is an individual concept: it applies to isolated acts.

Paul Strassman ("Information Payoff," Free Press 1985)

INFORMATION FLOW

A knowledge team's responsibility is to optimize information flows across departmental barriers. This runs against decades of corporate (and broad cultural) development that actively encouraged specialization and compartmentalization as a desirable end. The urban planner, Christopher Alexander, describes the old system as causing an "autonomy withdrawal syndrome." He means that greater and greater specialization of activities breeds withdrawal into smaller and smaller social units more and more insulated from one another.

The counterpoint to this trend is the belief that, rather than to limit contact, the *purpose of the organization is to maximize the opportunity for human interaction*. Since one purpose of human interaction is to exchange information, a corollary could be that *the purpose of the organization is, also, to mazimixe the opportunity for information exchange*.

The principle of "maximizing the *opportunity* for exchanging information" is a powerful socio-tech concept. To understand it, one can consider the opposite. What if one minimized the opportunity for human interaction and access to information? The author discovered the answer during travels to Moscow. It is almost impossible to make a telephone call, not only because there are fewer phones per person but because there are no phone books. The absence of a phone directory was [until recently] a deliberate effort by the government to minimize the opportunity for people to interact and to exchange information. The only people one can call are those whose numbers one happens to have. Clearly, no modern corporation could survive by making phone, fax, or E-mail numbers inaccessible.

The knowledge team is a corporate answer to optimizing the opportunity for human interaction and for exchanging information. The team is the depository and promoter of best practices in its particular domain. Answerable to the CEO, it judges the firm's effectiveness in the particular cross-function, whether product development, cost, delivery, or purchasing. In addition, it is responsible for continuous improvements in the particular cross function.

STRUCTURE

A formal structure of cross-functional teams provides a permanent means of coordinating vertical results and horizontal process (see Figure 7-2). This provides the CEO with *two* reporting structures:

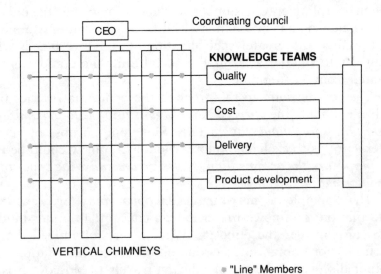

Figure 7-2 Vertical and horizontal structure

If there are many knowledge teams, they can be coordinated by a senior council chaired by the CEO. Hewlett–Packard's effort to establish corporate Product Generation Teams for hardware and software, described earlier in the book, is an example. Ford's Concept-to-Customer process, recently renamed World Class Timing, is a similar case. Dan Rivard, Ford's senior person responsible for CtC (and now WCT), coordinates a corporate team whose goal is to sharply cut down product-development cycle times. The focus is on mapping the most effective companywide process.

THE KNOWLEDGE TEAM
PROCESS "RECIPE"

The CEO empowers a senior executive to coordinate a corporate cross-function knowledge team with members from senior line positions. All key vertical parts of the corporate system (divisions or departments) are represented. Their mission is to optimize the interrelationship of the parts. If this means—by Ackoff's hypothesis—that "getting the corporation behaving as well as it can, none of the departments will be," then all team members must come to the table with open minds about their roles.

The problem, of course, is that traditional reward systems push the same executives to their limits in their vertical chimneys. Rewards must therefore be realigned to optimize corporate performance. Conflicts between group empowerment and vertical control can linger for decades. In his book, *The Fifth Discipline*, Peter Senge quotes at length a conversation between a company's senior executives representing research and development, marketing, sales, and manufacturing. It concludes with two telling comments by the head of sales and the manufacturing vice-president:

> SALES: Now, the other thing is that we're not communicating in any rich kind of way between marketing and R&D. As a matter of fact, it's getting more separate.... If we're going to work on the total needs of the customer...there has to be a way that's seen in a lot of different places in the company.

MANUFACTURING: You started off by asking why there is tension between R&D and marketing. You also have tensions between manufacturing and finance....To me it comes down to two words: "Empowerment versus Control." We tend to be a very control-oriented organization overall....Because they've got control and won't let me in, I'm going to go over here and do my own thing because I feel powerless to affect that at all.[4]

Conflicts such as this are rooted in decades and decades of command and control management methods. Protecting one's turf becomes reflexive. Unless the reasons for this behavior are addressed by the CEO, the company directors, or a corporate executive committee, it will not be possible or effective to manage process across corporate boundaries.

New performance incentives for executives must be rooted in total performance rather than departmental solo successes. When corporate goals take precedence over departmental ones, a cross-function team's mission can better juggle the interrelationships necessary to manage a process such as quality, cost control, delivery, purchasing, product development, or information management companywide. Since line managers are involved, the implicit assumption is that each member will balance his or her needs against those of others in order to optimize the whole system.

A knowledge team's work is not full-time. It meets periodically and, depending on the complexity of work being covered, may have staff assistance supplied by the team chairman. Its job is to *Plan* best processes and to *Check* the results of the process after it is implemented. In a PDCA (Plan Do Check Act) improvement cycle, the *Do* and *Act* belong to those with vertical responsibility to achieve results. This provides a full, continuous-improvement learning-and-feedback cycle.

The cross-function knowledge team's work product is a process "map" describing activities, events, phasing, standards, and information flows necessary to manage the cross function in question. Because the map reflects the thinking and needs of senior

KNOWLEDGE TEAMS

line people, it also represents their political "buy-in" into a total companywide process. In turn, it signals the divisional or departmental chimney that senior executives are committed to giving priority to companywide interests. The cross-function process map is mirrored hierarchically at divisional, departmental, and sectional levels of the organization.

This planning approach and the mapping technique was used at Eastman Kodak to manage its research and development. One problem it faced was that its twenty R&D groups were scattered worldwide among five major product lines. A corporate team determined that the most critical issue was to develop a R&D planning process. The team mapped an ideal process in a four fields format showing 8 key organizational players and 49 steps covering several months. Exit and entry criteria were written with customer needs in mind. According to Roger Cole, Director of Research and Management Resources, "the process [was] cycled [several times] and improvements were made with each cycle. ...From this overall master plan individual groups and boards proceed to develop implementation plans and processes for improvements with meeting the requirements of the output [exit] documents."[5]

This mapping process allowed Kodak to identify three critical R&D areas for improvement. One was to establish a *stewardship* process over critical technologies in order to better integrate technologies into the product groups. Another was the improvement of the *patent process* in order to maximize R&D investments. The third was to *shorten technology transfer turnaround* time.

Corporate knowledge teams, such as Kodak's, take a long checklist of factors into account before integrating them into a best practice process recipe.

IMPLEMENTING THE PROCESS RECIPE

The *Do* and *Act* steps of the PDCA cycle are executed by an implementation team with the mandate to produce results. These are action-minded "knowledge teams" with an eye to effecting improvement on actual projects. At Ford this might consist of product teams producing the Escort or Explorer vehicles. The *Plan* and *Check* steps are the responsibility of the *corporate* cross-function team that reviews implementation lessons and extracts improvements to the generic process models. The World Class Timing group at Ford is an example.

For the line people to function as a cross-functional team, organizational barriers between them must be eliminated and rewards instituted that support collaborative work. Strong leadership is a critical success factor. A product manager needs to be empowered to inspire and sustain a team's activities from beginning to end—however long the cycle. In some cases the leadership may be rotated phase by phase so that the individual with the most pertinent competence is in charge at the right time: a designer during the development phase, a production engineer during manufacturing, a sales executive during postproduction.

After unifying the team around well-understood and accepted goals, the leader will address "process" issues. If the teams' activity is product development, the corporate best practice recipe will be taken as a departure point. A process that is best for hardware will be very different from a software development process, or one oriented to creating a service product. Since the corporate recipe reflects line officers agreement on how they can best work together, it falls to the team to customize the recipe to fit their particular needs. New team members may be added, others taken out. Design reviews can be altered. Entry exit criteria may be amended. The team produces

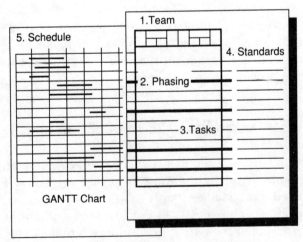

Figure 7-3 A four-fields process map

its own four-fields map and schedule as a blueprint for the project it will implement (see Figure 7-3). This preliminary planning stimulates teamwide communication by integrating all the process elements in the Checklist. In this manner, a proper work flow, concurrency of tasks, and information flows balance departmental activities necessary to both define and meet customer needs expeditiously. It allows, also, for building in a continuous-improvement review process.

Depending on the size and scope of the work, a knowledge team can be colocated in one building. DuPont Electronics brought together designers of a new connector cable technology to one site from dispersed locations. This allowed them to maximize both direct face-to-face contact and a richer information transfer. With the same intent, but on a vastly more complex scale, Boeing chose to colocate the members of 215 Design Build Teams working to develop the 777 aircraft. The purpose, too, is to reinforce each Design Build Team as a "knowledge team" in its own right by working face-to-face among themselves as well as face-to-face with other partner teams. A single site in Everett, Washington, will house many of these teams.

As it moves into deeper levels of component or subcomponent development, each knowledge team has its own process map linked upward to a master map "owned" by a core group. The goal throughout, however, is to optimize the whole. A "great" landing gear design for an aircraft may actually work at cross-purpose with a "great" hydraulic component design if one obstructs the functioning of the other. Compromises may actually result in a better concept for the total system. A minor example at Boeing was a Design Build Team's deliberations over a landing gear bay. The issue was a 5-inch space that was needed for a competing component. To meet both sides' ideal design, a bulge would have had to be created below the aircraft. This, in turn, would have had a drag effect measured in higher fuel consumption. The compromise sacrificed a preferred design feature on the landing gear in favor of another. Even though the landing gear team may have felt it lost, the total aircraft design benefitted.

Once planned out by a team, the actual process is monitored to record last-minute process improvements made on the fly. These are fed back to the corporate process knowledge team for checking and for incorporating changes in the basic process recipe. In this manner a reiterative PDCA cycle is sustained.

Because responsibility is delegated to a full team and not to isolated departments, a systemic process merges that optimizes the sum of the parts. An example is AAL, an insurance business with 1,900 field agents. To speed up processing, it organized multifunctional knowledge teams. "Under the new system, [the processing department] is divided into five groups, each serving agents in a different region. Each group consists of three or four teams of 20 to 30 employees who can perform all of the 167 tasks that formerly were split among three functional sections. Each team can handle all possible permutations involved in complicated cases."[6] For the agent it means one-stop shopping and a 20-day wait reduced to five days. For the company it means happier customers and the opportunity to eliminate a whole layer of middle managers who acquired different job responsibilities as the company grew. To encourage acceptance and employee improvement, a reward system was instituted for anyone who acquired new skills beneficial to a team.

Notes

Chapter 7

1. Peter F. Drucker, *Management: Tasks, Responsibilities, Practices*, Harper & Row, New York, 1974.

2. Confidential report by an MIT faculty person, Cambridge, Massachusetts, July 1990.

3. Dr. Russell L. Ackoff, "The Second Industrial Revolution," Undated paper, Wharton School, University of Pennsylvania.

4. Peter Senge, *The Fifth Discipline*, Doubleday, New York, 1990, p. 265.

5. Roger Cole, "Quality of Management of Research and Development," Kodak, Paper Presented at the Juran Institute, 1990.

6. "Work Teams Can Rev Up Paper-Pushers, Too," Business Week, November, 28, 1988.

8: FOUR-FIELDS MAPPING

Product development is very easy. But we have made it very hard for cultural reasons. It should be one system, one team, one set of decisions.[1] *Don Clausing (MIT)*

Four-fields mapping is one of the most elegant and productive techniques used by cross-function teams. It allows the members to determine in advance not only *who* does *what* and *when*, but also the flow of information, or *who needs to know what when*. This collaboration is a critical feature of a cross-function process. From the start, it forces team members to specify how they will identify and communicate customer requirements systematically both *across* vertical departments and suppliers.

Cross-function process mapping does not resemble any of the common *who-what-when* techniques such as time-driven GANTT schedules, work-breakdown structures (WBS), or PERT charts. All these tools, while they are useful for narrowly prescribed reasons, fall short in one significant way. None of these tools depicts horizontal relationships or the sharing of information essential to making companywide teaming work. This works against concurrency; the tools encourage compartmentalization of tasks and, in turn, sequential management. Anyone who has drawn a GANTT chart will quickly recognize this. It is only illusory that a total process can be managed through the financial or scheduling control of single activities. In reality there is little disciplined management going on because events are rarely linked other than through designated hand-offs. The tools perpetuate chimneylike task management.

The cross-function process map (see Figure 8-1) integrates four "information" fields:

1. The value-adding **team members** from all involved vertical chimneys

2. The breaking down of an activity into logical **phases**; clearly specified entry and exit criteria marking beginning and end points of each phase

3. Tasks to be performed and events such as decisions are **work flow** with special effort to depict horizontal concurrency and information sharing between team members at given points in time

4. Clearly delineated guidelines, regulations, or **standards** that are uniformly applied by all team members to activities and events

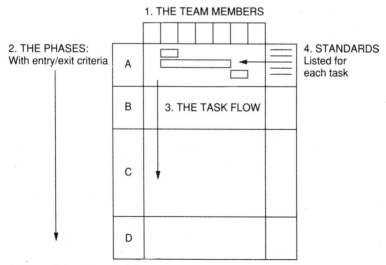

Figure 8-1 Four-fields map

The creation of a four-fields map is a unique and distinguishing feature of cross-function management, one the author first encountered at Komatsu. *The making of these maps helps stimulate the lateral communication that is widely acknowledged as a major shortcoming of conventionally managed companies.* Generic four-fields "maps" are created by a corporate knowledge team to control quality, cost, or product development processes; these are used as blueprints from which working teams can customize actual day-to-day implementation programs.

Four-fields maps are useful as a management resource but also as an organizational learning tool. As each map captures the learning of a prior effort, it becomes the departure point for the next effort. This contributes to a continuous–improvement process in a format that is easily communicable and transferable among teams.

A four-fields map depicts the process necessary to achieve a particular end result. Like a highway map that depicts the general interstate system and also has the blowup of a street layout in a city, a four-fields map is hierarchical in its detail. It shows a whole process at the highest level of generality and also windows into detailed elements. A well-managed company will eventually develop a book of corporate process maps, each one describing process methods, procedures, experiences, and relevant testing techniques.

Constructing a four-fields map may be the most creative communication exercise carried out by a companywide cross-function team. Just the act of talking together, which is done surprisingly little across chimney boundaries, is a revelation. "It is not unusual for the relationship between Design and Manufacturing personnel to be somewhat adversarial," says Larry Smith of Ford Motor Company. "Not long ago a Design Engineer (at Ford) stated 'Most product problems are a result of too much manufacturing variation.' A typical Manufacturing response, 'The Design is not robust.' It is an interesting exercise to ask Manufacturing and Design Engineers to identify the significant key characteristics of their product. On one particular occasion the two groups came up with totally different lists: one group not aware of why the other considered the list important."[2]

UP-FRONT TEAM PLANNING

When a child builds his or her first plane or ship model or tries a hand at a chemistry experiment, he or she learns a simple lesson. "Make sure that you have all the pieces laid out, the glue ready, the tools lined, and the plans read in advance." Advance planning is simple common sense especially if several departments are engaging in a complex process over a long period of time.

But the battle of budgets and schedules can kill the most ardent effort to plan diligently at the front end of a project or to lay out all the process elements in advance. The manager is invariably pressed to produce results fast. This means that he or she has very little patience with anyone or anything that might delay getting results.

Another roadblock is a tendency for "downstream" members of a team to think that early planning means extra work. "That's not something I was ever asked to do before," they will argue, "so why invent more meetings for me to attend?" This attitude misses the point. Becoming involved as team members early in a process actually lessens the work load for everyone. It does so by getting everyone to plan the process that will reduce errors and the need for rework.

Carefully executed up-front planning allows all team players to come to agreement on the customer requirements. It allows each one to identify advance information necessary to execute his or her role. The outcome of such communication—early in the process—is to minimize the flow of error downstream. The time spent doing it will pay itself back ten- to a hundredfold.

"What really makes the 777 project different," says Henry Shomber, one of the leaders in putting team process methods to work, "is the communication pathways that have been opened." A novelty at Boeing has been the Divisional general manager's insistence on getting the whole 777 team together for large meetings. In 1991 the team already consisted of 5,000 people. He does it by holding back-to-back sessions in a large theatre able to hold half the team at a time. "This helps cement the connection between the team and the corporate vision," says Shomber.

THE TEAM

The making of a four-fields map begins either by a CEO designating a team or by a CEO empowering a senior manager at a divisional or departmental level to lead a team (see Figure 8-2). The team may also include external members such as suppliers or customers. A core group of five to seven is often used as a rule of thumb for optimal size although many more team members may be involved at various times on specific tasks. The leader is empowered with the authority to select team members, to determine rewards, and to make go no-go determinations. The core group of successful cross-function teams will stay from the beginning to end of a full cycle of activities.

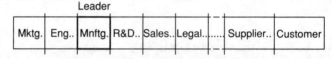

Figure 8-2 The team

Team members are chosen for the potential value they can add to a process. One does not include players, for example, whose only function might be to administer paperwork. In fact, one facet of the four-fields mapping process is to consciously strip out non-value-adding activity. Team players can include anyone from the CEO, to a sales account representative, to a technical expert, to an administrative secretary. This kind of representation is sometimes called "diagonal" because it cuts through all layers of a hierarchy.

PHASING AND ENTRY/EXIT CRITERIA

The first step in planning is to map the big picture, while carefully considering key decision points. Given precise project goals, a team can quickly break its efforts down into logical phases. Most companies have a generic corporate model of how to do this for various kinds of projects (see Figure 8-3). At GM the model is called the Four Phase, at DEC the six-step Phase Review Process, and at Xerox the eight-step Product Delivery Process. This phasing (see Figure 8-4) is a first breakdown of a process. Each phase concludes at a logical decision point, some-

Digital (generic)	Xerox (generic)
Phase 0 Strategy and Requirements	Preconcept Initiation
Phase 1 Planning and Preliminary Design (Business Plan)	Concept Initiation
Phase 2 Implementation and Design	Product Initiation
Phase 3 Qualification	Development Initiation
	Production Readiness Launch
Phase 4 Production, Sales, Service	Launch Go/Wait
Phase 5 Product Retirement (Service continues)	Product validation
	Fleet Upgrade (End of Life)

Figure 8-3 Phasing step examples

times called a *milestone* or *gate*. Depending on the uniqueness of the product, team members will eliminate, add, or amend the corporate four-fields blueprint. To be effective, those decisions should reflect the needs of *all* team players upstream and downstream. This is why their collective involvement in mapping the process is so important. It constitutes a "buy-in" to the decision making without which there would be serious errors or delays later. A milestone or gate associated with a phase is best controlled by specifying precise deliverables. Defined by the team itself, Entry/Exit Criteria (EEC) let all team members know exactly what shared information is needed to start a phase and what needs to have been accomplished collectively in order to exit it.

To "exit," customer requirements need to have been met. This is an important aspect of what makes *design reviews*—which are the events that determine whether exit criteria have been met—a vital management process control technique. If the review criteria are based on meeting customer requirements, and if all core team members sit in on a design review (instead of delegating that responsibility to a single chimney) the likelihood of meeting downstream needs and reducing rework is greatly increased. The reason is simple: the "downstream" person is sitting in on the review.

THE SEAMLESS ENTERPRISE

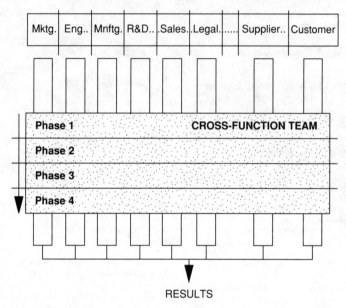

Figure 8-4 Phasing chart

EECs are formulated for each level of hierarchical planning (see Figure 8-5). A total project will have beginning and end criteria. A phase within the project will have its own criteria, and tasks within the phase will have their own criteria.

Why EECs? If designs are not well disciplined, errors or misjudgments can occur. The cost of repairing these errors or misjudgments escalates geometrically with time; the later you wait to repair it, the more there is to repair. The problem normally be-

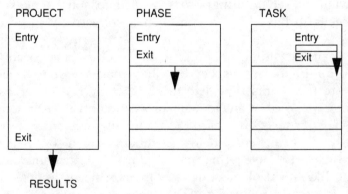

Figure 8-5 Entry/Exit Criteria (EECs) hierarchy

gins with someone having a *gut feeling* about a new product idea. Once the idea is translated into a design, it commits downstream effort to the execution of the design, the tooling of machines to build it, the preparation of manuals to teach users, and a sales campaign to sell it. If it is found too late that the originator of the product idea did not listen to customers, the product may not be saleable. In a fast-evolving product lines that can mean losing a one-time shot at a capturing a market niche.

Error and waste will occur in direct proportion to the lack of explicitness in EECs. Explicitness of EECs means that error and defects can be detected and the "process" causes corrected. This is accomplished by an inner Plan Do Check Act cycle designed to eliminate errors. Boeing planner, Al Viswanathan, terms this loop the *Error Prevention Process* (EPP), a methodology first conceived by Michael Fagan at IBM and used extensively in software engineering. No phase is exited until all detected errors and their causes are corrected.

This approach is anathema to schedulers because it is not time driven. Yet by giving precedence to meeting exit criteria over meeting the schedule, a company can greatly reduce the cost in time and dollars from correcting error and rework. Pilot efforts at Douglas Aircraft indicate the scale of the payoff. By using its own variation of the Error Prevention Process, it reduced engineering rework from 40 to 5 percent. Douglas estimated the return on investment of this improvement at 3–4:1.

Not all projects need to be disciplined this way. "Skunk works," unmonitored projects, are both creative and productive sources of new ideas. 3M gives many of its engineers and managers considerable free time to run their own skunk works. They are intentionally managed without formal scrutiny or justification. It is unlikely, however, that a company could survive by managing all its projects that way. Disciplined and replicable processes are needed to stay abreast of fast-moving markets and discriminating customers.

WORK FLOW

Once phase and entry/exit criteria are set, the team members are ready to collectively detail work flow tasks and relationships between them.

Tasks

A traditional task flow is sequential (see Figure 8-6). A single vertical chimney would define its own sequence of tasks. These would then be handed off to a neighboring chimney. Sequential flows do not have many horizontal links. Information and communication does not flow laterally between departments. This is generally accomplished through ad hoc meetings of multidisciplinary specialists. Many times meeting frequency is associated with successful teaming. "We meet once a week and really get along," is a frequent observation. No one stops to think that too many meetings may be a bad sign. How "few" times they meet might be a sign of better planning.

Depicted in this manner, tasks are often carried out independently of one another. This makes them easy to schedule. All one has to do is to estimate the time for each department's task and set a "begin/end" date. At the end date, a hand-off takes place to the next task or next chimney.

What inevitably happens is that a downstream hand-off results in rework because no one really bothered to ask what the downstream needs were. Time, money, and effort are lost.

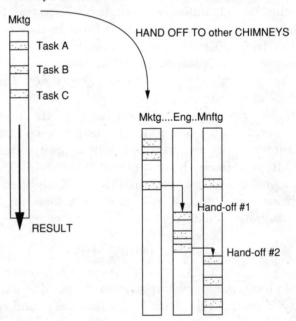

Figure 8-6 Traditional task flow

Mktg....Eng...Mnftg

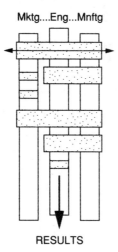

RESULTS

Figure 8-7
Concurrency

Concurrency

Concurrency is designed to minimize sequential hand-offs and to reduce the overall effort required in creating a design (see Figure 8-7). This is done by taking the sequential tasks outlined earlier and remapping them to include the early participation of downstream players. In our simple graphic example, single tasks are "stretched horizontally" to show shared activities such as Gather Customer Requirements. This might include a customer needs analysis jointly carried out by marketing, engineering, and manufacturing.

In this manner the process is mapped to show vertical and horizontal activities. For the process to work, careful thought must be given to the information flow connecting team members horizontally. The right information must be gathered, shared, reviewed, and translated into something of greater value.

Decisions, reviews, freezes

Once tasks have been mapped, decisions, milestones, or design reviews can be added as critical control points. EEC's are essential to making these review points effective. A design review is a teaming event that brings all affected players together to evaluate an idea before it is passed on (see Figure 8-8).

THE SEAMLESS ENTERPRISE

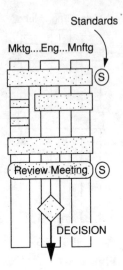

Figure 8-8   Review
meeting

Design reviews, like the movie director yelling "cut," are critical moments in letting a team anticipate "when to freeze" or call a halt to a particular design activity. This overcomes the temptation to keep designing until an idea is "absolutely right," which would result in a stream of costly engineering changes up and through production deadlines. During a car product-development program, for example, high costs are incurred by making numerous tooling changes. It is estimated that two-thirds of a $4 billion car program goes into retooling production equipment two or three times. Eliminating those changes so that only *one* tooling design process occurs can reduce a project cost by $1 billion or more and significantly shorten the time-to-market span.

Conventional product development permits engineering effort to escalate and peak, quite surprisingly, on the day that actual production line work starts. During those last days there is often a frenzy of design changes as engineers are finally pushed to meet a production deadline. Because of all the last minute changes, further design debugging alterations continue after production.

The timing of early prototypes and the freezing of particular design decisions around each prototype are effective methods for disciplining product development. They play a role in helping to reallocate valuable and scarce skills. By declaring a freeze, the team leader can allocate engineering effort more rapidly to the next phase. The empowerment of a team leader to make freeze decisions is a key component in disciplining the process.

Carefully managed freezes create a very different profile of engineering manpower usage. It peaks early. By the day of production, design changes are scaled down to zero. This allows scarce and highly paid engineers to begin work on new product-development cycles far sooner. In this manner an aggressive competitor, like a Toyota, can carry out several design cycles within a less efficient competitor's single cycle (see Figure 8-9). When comparing Japan, the United States, and European automobile producers, a team led by Kim Clark of Harvard Business School, found that both the United States and Europe used twice as many engineers as Japan per project.[3] Average engineering hours spent designing a car were three times lower for Japan, or 1,155 hours compared to approximately 3,500 for both the United States and Europe. These differences explain significant time-to-market advantages. In fast-moving product sector, such as the Fax machine sector, laptops, or workstations, these time-to-market advantages, derived from meticulous process management, are a critical success factor.

American firms are fast catching on to the importance of managing a product cycle to meet time-to-market pressures. The laptop and computer notebook business is an example. An American-engineered comeback is due to rapid product development turnaround by companies such as Compaq, Hewlett-Packard, and AST Research, Inc. NEC was put on the defensive when its notebook, based on an Intel 80386X chip, reached the market eight months later than its U.S. competitors' products. Toshiba, the market leader in laptops, found itself uncharacteristically constrained in the notebook market by its own inability to put the latest technology into its products.

STANDARDS (S)

Standards bring consistency to a process by ensuring that everyone is working with to the same customer requirements or the same design rules. *Intelligently specified standards help strengthen*

ENGINEERING DAYS

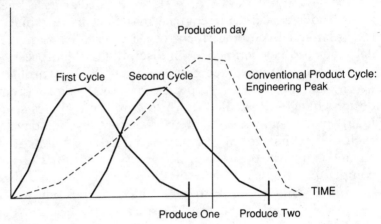

Figure 8-9   Engineering effort profile

horizontal communication by applying uniform information sharing across departmental boundaries. This is a central feature of the "warp and woof" analogy. The standard establishes the tightness of the weave, specifies the type of thread, and describes the pattern to be created. This brings far more unity to a team effort.

For a task entitled "**Gather Customer Requirements,**" a standard would prescribe the kind of information and data needed and how to format it so that it is useful to all team members. **Quality Function Deployment** (QFD) is an example of a standardized method of capturing and recording a team's understanding of customer requirements in a series of Quality Table (QT) matrices that plot needs (WHAT customers want) against the means of meeting them (HOW it can be achieved). (See Figure 8-10 and Chapter 9).

A Quality Table is an effective cross-function tool because, in order to complete it, team members must communicate needs and solutions intensively among themselves. As the next chapter suggests, this communication is often rated as the biggest single benefit of using QFD as a standardized method of understanding and meeting customer requirements.

Company product-development standards are highly proprietary. They constitute the secret ingredients of process discipline. There is very little proprietary information in telling a competitor

FOUR-FIELDS MAPPING

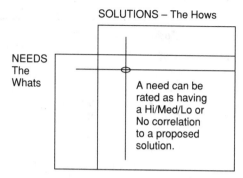

Figure 8-10   Quality table matrix

that a team will "Gather Customer Requirements." On the other hand, it would be of keen interest for that competitor to know the kind of information sought and the standards used to gather it. Standards can also include government regulations, company procedures, or design review methods. In an engineering-intensive setting, a list of testing and control standards is lengthy. The Institute for Defense Analyses developed a list of formal methods and the frequency each was used from a sampling of companies it studied (see Frequency/Method table).

SUMMARY

A four-fields process map is a unique planning tool. By integrating a variety of elements together, it provides a holistic beginning-to-end perspective. The technique is simple—no wallsize charts. It uses a hierarchical structure to detail or window into subparts as necessary. And it explains process in a clear, simple, graphic style—no thick word-laden reports.

The most evident payoff, as is true of many Total Quality Management tools, is *improved communication* brought about by engaging a whole team in discussions about goals and the best means of achieving them. The four-fields map is also a shorthand way of capturing the team's knowledge so that it can be continuously amended, improved, shared with other teams, or used as training tool.

The four-fields map is a fusion of all of the techniques introduced in this chapter: team leadership, hierarchical planning,

Frequency	Method
78	Graphs
43	Design of experiments
40	Pareto charts
40	Tree analysis and QFD
39	Cause & effect diagrams
36	Histograms
22	Scatter diagrams
18	Fault tolerance analyses [FTA]
13	Control charts
10	ANOVA
10	Computer techniques
9	Statistical test and elimination
8	Multiple regression
6	Relation charts
4	Failure Modes Effects Analysis [FEMA]

entry/exit criteria, design or prototype freezes, and process mapping. Together they provide the manager and his or her coworkers with a toolkit necessary for successful front-end planning. Through such process planning, a company can abide by the new competitive rules: customer-driven requirements, to continuous improvement, and concurrency.

A SAMPLE FOUR-FIELD MAP

A sample four-field map is presented below. This example from NEC IC-MiconSystem (NIMS) illustrates the evolution of its quality assurance *process map* between 1986 and 1987. In order to impose stricter control on the design process, NEC added two additional cross-functional design reviews. At the same time, the company eliminated several time-consuming product-planning tasks. Both changes resulted in a more efficient and effective chip-design process. Steps such as these were instrumental in allowing NEC to reach a point of getting its chip-design samples "right the first time" 99.9% of the time. This means that they can proceed directly to production without changes.

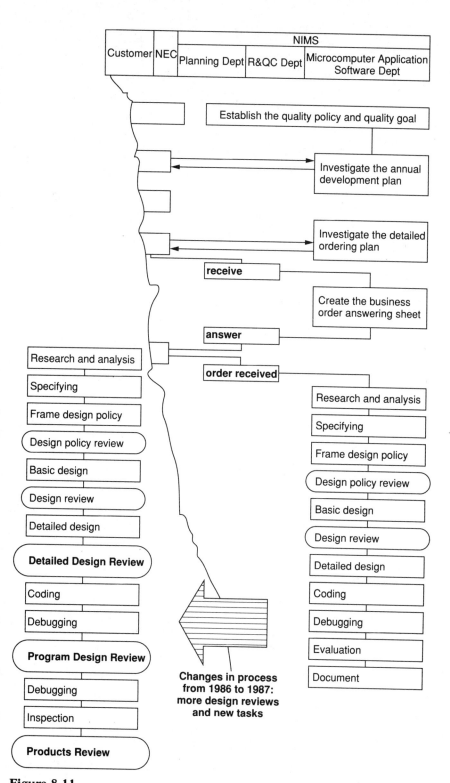

Customer	NEC	NIMS		
		Planning Dept	R&QC Dept	Microcomputer Application Software Dept

Establish the quality policy and quality goal

Investigate the annual development plan

Investigate the detailed ordering plan

receive

Create the business order answering sheet

answer

order received

Research and analysis	Research and analysis
Specifying	Specifying
Frame design policy	Frame design policy
Design policy review	Design policy review
Basic design	Basic design
Design review	Design review
Detailed design	Detailed design
Detailed Design Review	Coding
Coding	Debugging
Debugging	Evaluation
Program Design Review	Document
Debugging	
Inspection	
Products Review	

Changes in process from 1986 to 1987: more design reviews and new tasks

Figure 8-11

Notes

Chapter 8

1. Don Clausing, "Flexible Product Development," Speech at Owen School of Business, Vanderbilt University, Memphis, Tennessee, May 1991.

2. Larry Smith, "QFD and Its Application in Concurrent Engineering," Ford Motor Company, 1989.

3. Kim B. Clark, W. Bruce Chew, and T. Fujimoto, Working Paper: "Product Development in the World Auto Industry: Strategy, Organization, and Performance," April 1988, Harvard Business School, Division of Research.

9: NEEDS AND SOLUTIONS (QFD)

Every customer has *needs*. Low cost, high quality, and punctual delivery are among them. So is the need for features and other characteristics that are uniquely designed to a particular function or need. Companies, naturally, would like to satisfy them by devising *solutions* in the form of attractive products and services. This is, in fact, the heart of the competitive battleground worldwide. Ignore customer needs and the best machinery, information system, or sales force will do nothing to boost the fortunes of an enterprise.

But deciding exactly who is a customer is not always clear or simple, especially if the meaning is broadened to include anyone "next in line." This makes the job of defining and meeting customer needs suddenly more complex. Until recently there was no commonly accepted best way of understanding customer needs and arriving at solutions. Best practice was often simply someone's judgment, usually a designer or engineer or, in corporate terms, a marketing, design, or engineering department.

To deal with this complexity, better techniques had to be invented. This is what happened in Japan late in the 1960s when innovators set out to improve the way in which user needs are captured and then translated into precise, unambiguous instructions to designers and manufacturers. They soon discovered an important distinction. Customers can almost always express certain needs but there are many others that a customer does not know how to express or even may not know he or she has. The latter were referred to as latent needs.

Having arrived at this distinction, the same innovators set out to invent ways of systematically deploying an understanding of these needs across *all* departmental boundaries so that the optimal product *solutions* could be devised. The ideal goal of this exercise was to design and build no more and no less than desired by a customer. To do too much was a waste of time and money. Too little meant a loss of sales.

The method developed to do this, now diffused widely throughout Japanese firms and growing in use in the United States since its introduction in 1984, is broadly entitled Quality Function Deployment or QFD. Its principle management tool is a matrix called the Quality Table (QT), also known as the House of Quality because of the general shape given to the matrix. (See Figure 9-1). Customer needs are arrayed on one side against technical solutions on another.

"The goal is to transfer customer requirements or true quality characteristics into the quality of a final product or service," write two Japanese authorities, Tadashi Yoshizawa and Hisakazu Shindo. "This is done by translating the customer requirements into the appropriate technical requirements systematically for each stage of product development and production."[1]

Quality Tables are often confused in the United States with QFD. Quality Tables are a basic management tool; QFD, on the other hand, refers to a broad methodology for integrating customer requirements throughout all phases of a product-development process.

"Traditional market research techniques and procedures are not as much help...as you might think," says Robert Klein

QFD Methodology

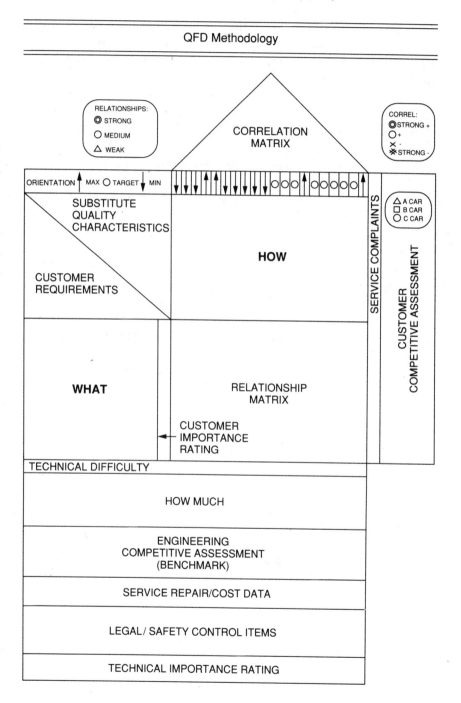

of Applied Marketing Science, Inc. "Where market research might ask customers about twenty or thirty product attributes, the Voice of the Customer in the [needs and solution] world will often consist of hundreds of attributes."[2]

A QFD process is closely linked to entry/exit criteria (EEC) in a four-fields template. In-depth analysis of customer needs provides many of the entry criteria; in the same manner solutions establish the exit criteria that must be met at any given point. These entry/exit criteria are essential for design reviews to errors before a milestone is bridged. Errors are of two kinds. One kind is related to technical performance; that is, the design simply does not work when tested. The other is related to customer needs—that is, are customer criteria adequately accounted for at predetermined decision points?

In a Quality Table matrix, "needs" are first expressed in the customer's own words and then translated into measurable characteristics. Thus, a requirement that a car be "silent" at high speed is translated into a decibel count. Solutions are the means for satisfying each requirement. The ensuing matrix is used to find an *optimal*

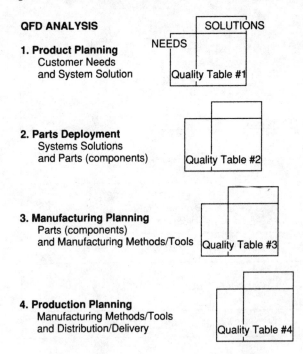

QFD ANALYSIS

1. **Product Planning**
   Customer Needs
   and System Solution

2. **Parts Deployment**
   Systems Solutions
   and Parts (components)

3. **Manufacturing Planning**
   Parts (components)
   and Manufacturing Methods/Tools

4. **Production Planning**
   Manufacturing Methods/Tools
   and Distribution/Delivery

SOLUTIONS
NEEDS
Quality Table #1
Quality Table #2
Quality Table #3
Quality Table #4

combination of needs and solutions necessary to create a delighted customer. Needs can be prioritized and only those most important to the customer can be addressed. A cascading sequence of Quality Tables can run through a full product development cycle stage-by-stage. One example is a generic four-step sequence that progresses from product planning to production advocated by the American Supplier Institute in Dearborn, Michigan. A far more complex web of quality tables is proposed by a nonprofit consulting group called GOAL/QPC in Methuen, Massachusetts. It advocates an arrangement called the Matrix of Matrices that includes thirty different tables. No company in the United States is known to have actually used all thirty in a single program. NEC in Japan is the only company that the author is aware of that has attempted such a complex QFD analysis.

Once user needs have been detailed and understood, it is then determined how well competitors are meeting each of those requirements. This allows a product team to make a strategic decision on which customer requirements to emphasize in a new product. A further level of analysis can be added by establishing the degree of difficulty involved in achieving a solution. Since solutions often are defined in technical terms, the difficulty may involve developing a completely new technology or improving an existing one. A completed Quality Table integrates a complex array of competitively useful information into a simple format.

To arrive at this level of analysis in a single table, a cross-departmental team must collaborate in gathering data, integrating it into a matrix, and deducing a preferred product solution from the overall picture. This requires the team to communicate openly and extensively. The team develops a consensus on goals, needs, and solutions, and the company then strives to reach the goals, fill the needs, and implement the solutions. As a result, time-to-market is reduced, product development costs are lowered through less rework, and the final product or service is more satisfying to the customer.

DEC's first efforts with QFD-styled analyses started in 1986 after Lou Cohen took an introductory course offered by a quality management consulting company. This led him to initiate several

QFD AT DEC

One of the pioneers of the QFD process in the United States is Lou Cohen, a program manager at Digital Equipment Corporation. He devised a short but effective two- to three-day process for creating a Quality Table.
Implementation Techniques:
Prework: *Get the voice of the customer*
    customer participates
    contextual inquiries (in user's work context)
    written results of phone surveys
    user group experiences
    problem reports

Prework: *Plan the Needs/Solution process*
    define the key customers
    define the time-span covered by Needs/Solution
    determine the participants
    determine logistics (place, time)

Day One
    do affinity diagram of customer needs
    rank order customer needs
    do affinity diagram of solution features

Day Two
    correlate needs and solutions
    rank order solution features
    prepare action plan

Source: Presentation to the International Association for Electronic Product Development (IAEPD), July 25, 1991 at AT&T Bell Labs.

trial efforts. The first, said Cohen, was a case "of the blind leading the blind." One of the major stumbling blocks included an open-ended timetable to complete the Quality Table, an uncertain market definition, and an unstable organization with halfhearted participants. By the third attempt, a group of fifteen senior managers successfully participated in building a Quality Table matrix for the VAX 9000. Major benefits surfaced. In Cohen's words, "the entire program team ended up with *a common vision* of the product. In addition, everyone got a fair hearing. People were able to accept key trade-offs even though they did not like them. And lastly, the range of customer needs was wide but well understood."

These experiments, increasingly successful, gained credibility for the QFD approach at DEC. Within two years forty teams had used it for applications ranging from strategic marketing, to software, hardware, services, and organizational planning. The company has since lost count of how many efforts have been initiated. As to QFD benefits, Lou Cohen offers a six-point summary:

1. It helps prioritize work/features.

2. It is a team-building tool.

3. It forces the asking of embarrassing questions.

4. It means that people share their viewpoints because they have a need to come to consensus.

5. It motivates engineers to meet face-to-face with customers.

6. It expands the team's view of the *total* product to include such things as training, service, and packaging.

A similar evolution occurred at AT&T. After hearing about the process from a presentation by DEC's Lou Cohen, an internal team went to work and successfully completed a single Quality Table. By 1991, almost sixty were completed in various parts of AT&T and customized training materials were developed for in-house groups. In contrast to DEC, however, AT&T's initial trial efforts consumed far more time and effort. One Quality Table analysis took seven months to evolve. During that time four people, on average, worked together for more than 200 hours and a cumulative individual time of 1,100 hours. Despite the considerable effort, the experiment was considered well warranted. "We learned that understanding the customer voice strengthens the organization," said Susan Brown, a member of the technical team propagating QFD methods at AT&T. "We strengthened the team while making much more explicit the reason for the product. This builds credibility with customers. In addition, we accumulated a rich, accessible product definition database."

Experiences similar to DEC's and AT&T's are echoed by Harold Schaal, a pioneering figure in propagating QFD methods at Ford Motor Company. "Without the voice of the customer as a key operating principle," he says, "the decision as to when and where to use powerful analytical tools such as Taguchi's Design of Experiments is left to the voice of the engineer or executive." More than 400 "Voice of the Customer" Quality Tables have been developed since 1984 when Don Clausing of MIT introduced the concept to managers at Ford, the first U.S. company to apply them.

Says Schaal, "Our QFD efforts are now distributed in three directions, each having evolved in an uncoordinated manner. One is focused on making components design more tightly linked to assembly. This uses the standard four-stage approach advocated by the American Supplier Institute. Another, customized by Ford, is focused on linking the engineer more closely to the customer. And a third is focused on Car Program planning. The latter is a Ford innovation which we have not seen anywhere in Japan's auto industry, even though they use QFD extensively for component and subsystems design."

In Japan, the most prolific user of QFD is Nippon Electric Company (NEC). Its IC-Micom System (NIMS), a subsidiary supplying almost 70 percent of its parent company's integrated chip designs is illustrative. By year's end in 1990, a decade after its founding, it had completed 2,000 Quality Table analyses. Most of these zoom in on discrete IC design problems. The matrices count not more than 30 items on each axis.

One sign of the impact of QFD on improving the design of IC chips is measured in the "hit rate," or the number of times the customer-desired design is correct the first time. It was lifted from only six out of ten a few years earlier, to 99.9 percent even though chip design complexity has risen geometrically. Patient and ongoing application of Quality Table analyses is considered a principal cause of this improvement. This persistence is attributed to the recently retired president, Kiyoshi Uchimaru, who personally mastered QFD and taught the process to his staff and employees.

Another user, but one with a different approach, is the Japan System Corporation, a producer of major software programs for large clients such as utilities. Its president, Yoshiaki Katayama, who is a strong advocate of QFD, urges his employees to use simple Quality Tables to diagnose and resolve complaints that may come from a utility client. This focuses a team's attention on a specific problem with the goal of arriving at a quick solution. A team's use of QFD methods is left to their discretion. "I am a role model," says Katayama, "but I do not insist they use it."

Quality tables can be created for any variety of other uses. Procter & Gamble Co. uses them to devise new linkages with its high-volume discount houses, an application not seen in Japan. Volvo uses them to strategize corporate plans. The author is planning to use the techniques in a political campaign in order to optimize a set of policy proposals. QFD methods are being applied innovatively in the management of software engineering. In the latter case, innovative Quality Table techniques were introduced in mid-1991 to the International Association for Electronic Product Development (a consortium of 14 U.S. electronic firms) by the CSK Corporation, Japan's largest independent software development company. One of its innovations was to change the basic four-step sequence of matrix correlations in order to accommodate software user requirements that are often difficult to express or translate into precise technical solutions. CSK, in addition, is the first company to apply complex quantification methods to help prioritize combinations of requirements and solutions within the matrix. This allows them to focus on single elements that are of major importance and not waste time on those of secondary value.

Three important points highlight the benefits of QFD. The most important attribute of QFD is that the basic exercise of creating Quality Tables induces intense cross-departmental communication between all members of a team. Second, it provides a disciplined method for capturing and recording actual and latent customer requirements and the ways in which they will be satisfied. This record can be used to rapidly reiterate new cycles of product improvements. And lastly, it pushes the imperative of being customer driven down into each phase of the product-development process. QFD provides managers and workers with a structured method for conceiving solutions without losing sight of the totality of the process.

Notes

Chapter 9

1. Tadashi Yoshizawa and Hisakazu Shindo, *Quality Deployment in Software Product Development*, ICQC, Tokyo, 1987, p.485.

2. Robert Klein, Presentation Published by the Second Symposium on Quality Function Deployment, GOAL/QPC, Boston, December, 1989.

PART III
BREAKING SILOS

Mechanistic systems (sc. 'bureaucracies') define [individual] functions, together with the methods, responsibilities, and powers appropriate to them; in other words...boundaries are set. In being told what he has to attend to, and how, he is also told what he does not have to bother with...what he can post elsewhere as the responsibility of others.

In organic systems, the boundaries of feasible demands on the individual disappear. The greatest stress is placed on his regarding himself fully implicated in the discharge of any task appearing over his horizon, as involved not merely in the exercise of a special competence but in commitment to the success of the concern's undertakings.

Tom Burns ["The Management of Innovation," Tavistock Publications, London, 1961, p. viii.]

10: THE PACESETTER

Team Taurus, Ford Motor Company's bet-the-house automobile program, was America's first major effort to challenge a legacy of managing through a pyramid of departmental silos. Led by Lewis Veraldi, Team Taurus spanned a six-year period from 1980 to 1986. When I was first introduced to Veraldi's team and to the curvacious prototypes early in their evolution, it was evident that something significant was happening. Ford's gamble was that solutions would be found as much by reinventing its management methods as in making technical advances in styling—such as flush windows—or modernized production tooling. The gamble was on Ford's people and their ability to work as a team.

What Veraldi represented was the Americanization of methods and techniques that he had already started to institute in Ford's European operations during the 1970s. Just as important was that these same methods had already been institutionalized in Japan decades earlier by Toyota and later at Mazda, Ford's

Japanese partner. Veraldi was also ready and willing to learn from Japan. Ford executives and labor representatives made many trips to Japan during the 1980s.

For the reader, Toyota Motor is a good place to begin to understand what is meant by cross-function mangement. The story starts sixty years ago rather inauspiciously. Toyota's first try at making a car was based on an engine design sketched from a 1933 Chevrolet and a body appearance copied from the lines of a 1934 Chrysler DeSoto. The frame and rear axle were lifted from a Ford; the front axle from a Chevrolet. This hybrid concept yielded a total of three cars before the company moved on to the next model. Later, as the war economy mushroomed, trucks were seen as a far bigger commercial opportunity, and car development was sidelined. This time a Ford truck model was copied and produced in large quantities. By necessity, the truck chassis became the basic structure for Toyota's cars. It was only in 1950 that the company was ready to produce a first for Japan: a car *not* built on a truck frame and chassis.

Desperately needing to radically modernize and improve operations in order to keep with a surge in postwar growth, Toyota chose to inspire its own methods of production rather than simply copy Western methods. It shopped around for ideas. The American technique of stocking supermarkets on an as-needed basis, only when the shelves needed refilling became the foundation of Toyota's now famed "just-in-time" (JIT) system. Parts were sent to production only as needed rather than being inventoried in large stockpiles. Internal component flow was managed by the company's innovative "kanban" ordering process. In 1965, only thirty years after building its first car, the company received the Deming prize for its quality management system. A major reason for the award was the recognition of Toyota's innovative method of managing horizontally across departments and suppliers.

The payoffs of the company's disciplined and consistent improvement process are phenomenal given the starting point. By 1990 it was exporting one million cars to the United States, fourth in total volume behind the big three. The *Lexus*, a car whose product-development manager personally inspected 2,000 design drawings to check their conformance to his original concepts, established itself as a price and performance match for Mercedes and BMW.

The company, first established in 1918 as Toyoda [spelled with a "d"] Spinning and Weaving, was termed the "best car company in the world" by *Fortune* magazine.[1] In 1991, J. D. Powers, the noted scorekeeper on user ratings of cars, listed the Toyota *Lexus* number one for quality, service, *and* selling methods. One of the factors that was most important in bringing the company to this pinnacle was the *TQM* system that it pioneered. Two broad, interwoven features of this system, its cross-functional techniques and its long-range policy planning, are explained below.

CROSS FUNCTIONS AND POLICY

Cross functions were instituted, as was noted in the Origins chapter, as a way of coordinating both departments and a wide network of suppliers dispersed principally throughout Nagoya, Toyota's home city and production center. First put into place in 1962, they evolved into a well-oiled companywide system of process management. This process was described in a book by Kenji Kurogane, the first Japanese to author, in 1988, a book on cross-function management.[2]

Cross-function practices at the parent company, Toyoda Automatic Looms Works, Ltd. [successor to Toyoda Spinning & Weaving], are implemented through a series of companywide *governing councils* (if literally translated from the Japanese they would be termed "conferences") bridging the six main corporate divisions. Each division, of which Toyota Motor is one, has its own cross-department councils. Each council concentrates on a single cross-function issue such as cost control or quality assurance. The purpose is to coordinate actions across the divisions or across departments. This network of cross-function councils is called by Toyoda "The Cross-Function Control System." A coordinating body for these councils reports directly to the Managing Director. With divisional executives sitting on this group, conflicts between each cross-function council are discussed and resolved so that they collectively work to achieve *corporate strategic goals*. Division-level cross-function teams report to the corporate council, which is also responsible for establishing policy directives; subdepartment teams report to the division team.

A ten-year long-term Management Plan is the guiding force behind the work of the cross-function councils. A tangible expression of the corporate *vision,* the Plan lays out product plans and the cross-function requirements in such areas as quality, cost, and delivery. This allows the formulation of five-year and annual plans that the whole corporate entity works to fulfill. All plans are revised every year to reflect external factors, changes in performance, and new ideas from management. The process of revising them is described in a *four-fields* format expressed in PDCA phases. (See Figure 10-1).

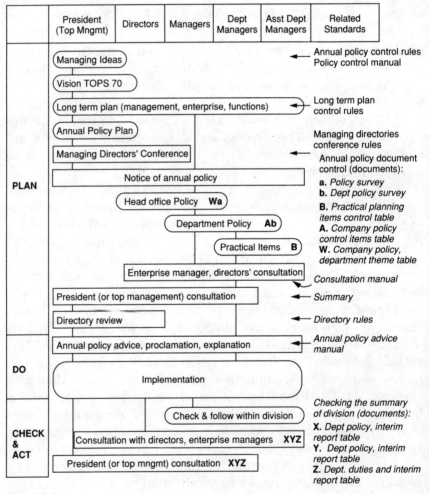

Fig. 10-1

The **team** field shows the organizational layers involved in the process from the president down to assistant department managers. The **phase** field is depicted both as a PDCA cycle and as a group of sequential stages that includes planning, developing, implementing, checking, and following. **Task flow** is depicted with symbols. In many cases single tasks are drawn to show the inclusion of several players horizontally in the execution of the task. Feedback loops are indicated with dotted lines. In the **standards** column are listed all pertinent guidelines and manuals. They are linked to actual tasks with a key letter: a, b, A, B, W, X, or Y. The four-fields format provides a simple graphic method for depicting the interaction of team players. At a single glance one can check the "white space" to see who is or is not included in any activity.

A process map depicting coordination of long-term and annual plans is called the Policy Control Cross-Function System. Each year, planning is cascaded down into each division, its departments, and their vertical functional chimneys. Uniformity is achieved by requiring that all documentation meet the same degree of specificity outlined in eight annual policy documents. The process eliminates potential conflict of policies, capital investments, production, and delivery goals at all levels of the corporation. Coordination of policies and goals is left to divisional managers and their president.

Cross-function control and policy management are used to enlarge the communication links between all levels of the corporation and to unify everyone in meeting common goals.

PRODUCT DEVELOPMENT
AS A CROSS FUNCTION

Product development is treated as a cross function by each division. The goal is to link planning, design, marketing, and manufacturing by interweaving functional tasks concurrently. This is illustrated by the example of a new forklift project, the X-300, in which the aim was to achieve, in Toyota's words, *extremely high quality*.

The project team started by establishing several targeted goals: a high-quality vehicle with the fewest possible design changes, a shorter time-to-market, and lower costs. *Improved communication* was seen as the key to achieving these goals during each of the project's three main phases: planning, designing, and manufacturing. Six steps were outlined to achieve these goals.

1. *Review both the divisions' long-term and annual plans.* This ensures that the team's product idea conforms to the overall direction being taken by the company.

2. *Prepare a process plan that conforms to the recommended corporate four-fields process map for minimizing warranty cost.* (Figure 10-2).

More complex than the policy control process map, the corporate four-fields process map arrays eight core players as the **team**. (It is notable that one player is loosely termed "market.") The **phasing** includes the three main project phases as well as follow-on into mass production, sales and service, and checking for feedback and

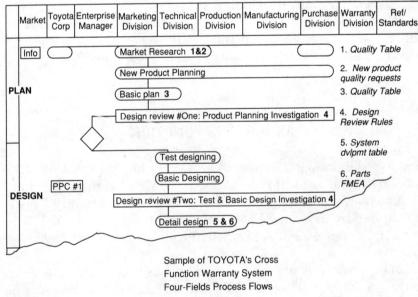

Sample of TOYOTA's Cross
Function Warranty System
Four-Fields Process Flows

Figure 10-2

improvement. The **task flow,** at this level of generality, is simple and straightforward. It is the highest-level overview of the whole project. Subsequent four-fields maps might be drawn to detail specific tasks.

One of the map's unique features is the inclusion of eight key design reviews involving five principal vertical chimneys. This ensures strong lateral communication at decision points, a key to effective cross-function management. Each design review is tagged with the number 4 pointing to a standard (in the right column) entitled "Design Rules." This is a corporate methodology spelling out the ways in which to carry out a successful design review. [See Item 3 below.]

Under the team player headed "Toyota Motor Corp" are several references to activities labeled "PPC 1,2,3,4." These refer to the division's Product Planning Council whose responsibility is to monitor and continuously improve the four-fields process map.

The **standards** column (right-hand side) lists all process guidelines and methods. Each one references a corporate document spelling out procedures, information needs, and test methods. Quality Function Deployment is called for under numbers 1, 2, 3, and 10 as Demanded Quality Development Table, New Product Quality Requests, and Quality Table. The total listing of standards is a proprietary resource of great value to the company. Its importance is similar to a football team's "playbook," or a military officer's book on combat techniques. The standards are treated as a dynamic resource constantly altered to reflect the changing requirements and needs of a process team. (This contrasts with many U.S. company "standards" books that are written by a corporate staff and remain unchanged for many years).

3. *Establish* **a strong design review** *process through each phase.* This is done by having the team collectively define clear *entry/exit criteria* for each phase, by using the review process to prevent problems from migrating downstream

in order to permit timetables and cost goals to be met, and by creating a design review checking procedure that allows problems to be detected, analyzed, and corrected as soon as they occur.

4. *Check regularly on whether the product meets customer requirements.* Quality Tables are used as a valuable reference point against which to measure progress in meeting user requirements. Ongoing contact with customers is also recommended.

5. *Implement specific improvements in each development phase.*

   PLANNING PHASE: Making product planning customer responsive by using market segment data to help define the product; using Quality Tables in order to establish the key Sales Points as well as Quality Goals and to involve both technical and non-technical functions in defining the customer requirements and product definition.

   DESIGNING PHASE: Keeping product design on target by using company-specified Test Design Investigations, Order Shift Investigation, and Order Plan Investigation methods to monitor the level of achievement, and conducting preinspections where new functions are being introduced to the vehicle by using company-specified Future Functional Evaluation, Failure Modes Effects Analysis (FMEA), and customer research methods.

   MANUFACTURING PHASE: Improving the manufacturing processes with preinspection, feature guarantees, FMEA, and personnel planning and training.

6. *Implement Product Design Investigation within all related divisions as part of the design review process.*

THE X-300 PROJECT

Working within these six process guidelines, the X-300 forklift project team established two primary customer requirements: product endurance and a long lifespan. To better monitor its product design, the team developed an On Board Acceleration Endurance Test to match customer-defined standards against the product. Special attention was given in this project to gathering detailed technical data on competing products and incorporating the findings into the design throughout the product-development phase. This allowed the team to establish the marketable life-span for the X-300 and not waste design time trying to exceed the span— or underestimate it and lose customers.

Through ongoing studies of its testing procedures, the team decided that the overall Test Car Evaluation methods based on customer specifications did not meet benchmarking requirements against competitors. It devised an improved evaluation system that included more of both Toyota customers and competitors' customers in the testing of trial vehicles. This allowed adjustments to the design that would provide characteristics superior to competitors' products. And, in order to maintain a product design of the highest quality, a "perfect" preinspection and evaluation was required of all design reviews.

The team's focus on process management and improvement, coupled with its engineering design skills, led to a successful introduction of the X-300. For senior managers, the project's success reconfirmed the importance of customer needs being interwoven from the very beginning into the definition of product quality. This led to a minimum of design changes, thereby saving time and money.

While no one would expect to carbon copy a management formula that is designed to fit the unique corporate culture nurtured by the Toyoda family, many of the elements of the TQM model applied by Toyota and summarized in the graphic overview in Chapter 10 are transferable to U.S. companies. Many of them, surprisingly, were once well known to American managers. Fifty years ago, George Hyde listed a number of fundamental principles in his 1946 edition of the *Fundamentals of Successful Manufacturing*.[3]

1. Have product designers and process developers work closely together.

2. Pay careful attention to appearance of design.

3. Develop a policy of never-ending improvement in the product; augment it by research and good lab facilities; and have a program of new product development.

4. Stay flexible; never establish something with the idea that it is permanent; anything can be improved.

5. On mechanization: think of tools and mechanization as means of employing labor to better advantage.

6. Be precise in process design and definition; use process charts; record the know-how; balance your lines.

7. Be a bear about cleanliness; don't accept dirt as a way of life.

Toyota delivered on each of these American-originated principles.

Two other corporate case examples follow. They profile American companies, Boeing and Digital Equipment, that are taking the first steps to rediscover and incorporate these principles into their day-to-day operations.

Notes

Chapter 10

1. "Why Toyota Keeps Getting Better and Better and Better," *Fortune*, November 19, 1990.
2. The material in this chapter is based on case material described in the book *Management by Cross Function*, edited by Kenji Kurogane, Japan Standards Association, Tokyo, 1988. Translation privately commissioned by the author by permission of JSA.
3. In Robert H. Hayes, Steven C. Wheelwright, and Kim B. Clark, "Dynamic Manufacturing," Free Press, New York, 1988, pp. 52–53.

11: CONCURRENT ENGINEERING

In 1990, Boeing broke with tradition. For the first time its commercial division applied concurrent engineering methods to the design and assembly of a new aircraft, the 777. The decision challenged a legacy of compartmentalized habits and corporate practices.

The complexity and scale of the management innovations to be undertaken was boggling. This is difficult enough, but the company decided also, in tandem, to design the whole airplane electronically on 3-D computer systems. One hundred and thirty thousand engineered pieces are being integrated electronically, ready for manufacture and assembly to take place. Advanced "CATIA" software developed by the French aerospace industry is the main computer design tool. IBM mainframes and Cray computers anchor the enormous data flows of thousands of high-powered workstation terminals linked together.

CONCURRENT ENGINEERING

By deciding to use 3-D electronic-design methods, Boeing committed itself to a breakthrough. Merely by "going electronic," Boeing insured that the design and management processes would never be the same again. The 3-D technology called for new teaming concepts. By linking engineering disciplines together "on-line," designers were pushed to develop a new method of cooperative teamwork. This challenged the core of what was considered the normal way of working: "I'll do my thing and send it to you when it's ready. After that it's your problem." With the 3-D system design and assembly specialists could look in on each other's work simultaneously months before it would usually occur under conventional methods.

An unprecedented agreement by senior *engineering* executives (one chimney) and *manufacturing* executives (another chimney formally called Operations) set the stage for specialized engineering disciplines to work as a single product team for the 777. This agreement meant that Boeing Commercial would not be the same again. The respected magazine *Aviation Week & Space Technology* touted the changes with the headline "777 Revolutionizes Boeing Aircraft Development Process."[1]

CHANGE AT BOEING

A core team with members from specialized departments drawn from Engineering and Operations oversaw five key Design Build Teams (DBTs), each responsible for a major component of the aircraft. Under them were specialized DBTs focusing on subsystems, components, and parts: more than 215 teams in all. The author's experience working with several 777 Design Build Teams early in the program's start-up phases highlights some of the management challenges facing Boeing.

Traditionally, an aircraft design starts with structures specialists designing the shell of the plane. There, concepts are translated into a full-scale wooden mock-up. When the mock-up is finished, other specialists in hydraulics or electrical systems enter the design cycle. They proceed to negotiate design alterations that accommodate each one's needs: space here for some hydraulic lines, bypass there for some wires, more space for a landing gear

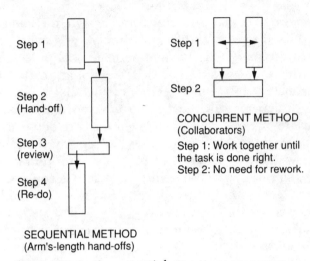

Step 1

Step 2
(Hand-off)

Step 3
(review)

Step 4
(Re-do)

Step 1

Step 2

CONCURRENT METHOD
(Collaborators)
Step 1: Work together until
the task is done right.
Step 2: No need for rework.

SEQUENTIAL METHOD
(Arm's-length hand-offs)

Figure 11-1 A sequential versus a concurrent process

assembly. The old process was sequential, with each step leading to a hand-off to the next.

The new process is significantly different (see Figure 11-1). For the 777, specialists were asked from the very first day to work within colocated teams and to work without a full-scale wooden mock-up. This allowed tasks to be carried out concurrently, meaning that one activity was not waiting for a prior to be finished before itself getting started. The fact that specialists sat "colocated" side-by-side with sophisticated electronic systems hooking them up facilitated the process.

Questions soon cropped up, and lessons were quickly learned. Authority was an immediate issue. Did a design team leader have the authority to require attendance at a meeting from engineers who were not used to entering the design cycle at the beginning? Who would decide when a design was ready? What techniques could be used to force concurrent design discussions—and what did concurrency mean anyway? Since people were being colocated what were they supposed to do differently? What information were they required to share? The initial DBT efforts were launched without answers. They were the pilot teams, *learning by doing.* This process that was instituted emulated the PDCA (Plan, Do, Check, Act) cycle of reiterated improvements. The SDCA

(Standardize, Do, Check, Act) runs parallel to the PDCA. The latter focuses on continuous improvement through short cycles (four months or less). The former, SDCA, takes each improvement and standardizes it.

This, it turned out, was a challenge more subtle than it first appeared. Team members did not always show up for meetings thereby challenging the team leader's authority. Guidelines for how to work as a team had to be created. Even a new terminology had to be invented to account for additional degrees of electronic-design detail that were not possible with simple paper drawings.

A more onerous hurdle, however, was plain and simple economic reality. Boeing had signed-on paying customers for 777 and the fuse was burning. Because Boeing promised to build a "customer-preferred" airplane, a big part of this commitment was to deliver a service-ready airplane on time. The pressure of a clock ticking was felt as soon as initial orders were taken from All Nippon Airways and United Airlines and delivery dates promised.

Accounting and Scheduling, two traditionally powerful "chimney" functions, reasserted a familiar number-driven management style. First, budget controls were tightened. This meant that very little front-end time could be spent by teams to detail concurrent engineering procedures and plans. Since such a planning effort might take one to three weeks depending on the complexity of the team's design assignment, accountants computed the cost in time and effort. By the author's informal estimate the math added up to the following: 220 teams × 15 people per team × an average of 7 full working days in planning meeting × $250 per day in salary and benefits = $5,775,000. These were big numbers to cost-accountants who had no way of determining accurate estimates of the benefits that might come from careful advance planning. More onerous was Scheduling. In the aerospace industry, schedulers are the "heavies." Their job is to manage WBS or work breakdown structure, that is, the breakdown of a project into the minutest work tasks, and then to date each task with beginning and end times. The outcome is a set of wall-sized master schedules with thousands of neatly labeled activities and events. Most often these schedules showed sequential step-by-step task management: such and such task precedes such and such, and so on. Rarely, if at all, do these scheduling maps show lateral or "concurrent" connections between activities. Since those are not really quantifiable, they "don't count." Deadlines do, and these dictated who would do what and when, task-by-task. Managers, by the old rules, had the responsibility of imposing the deadlines.

Unfortunately, concurrency challenges the basics of what schedulers do. When two tasks are managed "concurrently," the actual time needed to complete is not really the important variable. Rather, it is the quality of the information exchanged that is important. This is how design error and rework is eliminated. On the other hand, if time is the determinant, tasks will be completed without eliminating errors that might be detrimental to someone later. In such a case the overriding priority is to meet the delivery date—no matter what. Concurrency in the process is intended to balance the drive to meet customer needs of quality and cost and tight delivery.

Boeing executives had hoped to reduce error and rework. The only way to do this, as was described in the Toyota X-300 case, is to hold back on key decision points until the design was right. Otherwise unfinished or incorrect designs might be handed down. Delays "to get it right" were not only not part of the old rules, but they were anathema to classically schooled schedulers. Under those rules, engineers admitted privately, it was not unusual in the aircraft industry for drawings to be authorized without proper checking for completeness just to "meet the schedule." Everyone knew that there was always time to fill them in later. That indeed was the way things worked. It did not mean that the final product suffered—Boeing's commercial aircraft are the best in the world— but only that extensive design rework was a costly part of the system.

The social and organizational complexity to be reengineered was enormous as the scheduling bias indicates. Equally daunting to integrate was a multidimensional organizational structure. This was not simple old-fashioned matrix management. As the chart in the exhibit indicates, the new Design Build Teams represent only one organizational dimension that is supported by three other specialized structures: the engineering organization (in the left-hand column), nonengineering organizations (in the right-hand column), and specialized technical functions for various subsystems (in the bottom row). Each reflected habits belonging to compartmentalized silos reflecting specialized disciplines, different management, and different reward systems.

SECTION 41*

The initial planning efforts of one Design Building Team named Section 41, provide a window into the process of instituting new working methods. Section 41 is a subpart of the DBT responsible for the body. It is one of five high level design groups that constitute a full aircraft team. The other four include the wings, assembly (which brings all the physical elements together), empennage (which focuses on the tail assembly), and the power pack and strut (which encompasses all the engines). (See Figure 11-2.)

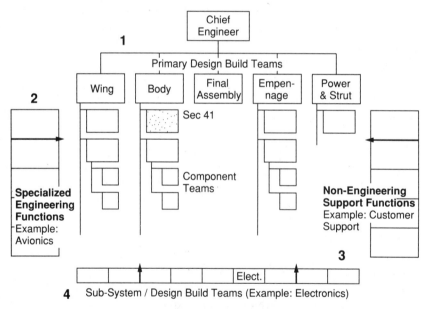

FOUR DIMENSIONS OF TEAMING AT BOEING

Figure 11-2

* Insights and judgments on the activities of Section 41 are the opinion of the author based on his experiences as a cross-function teaming consultant to Boeing Commercial's New Airplane Division. These views are not represented as those of the Division.

Section 41's first innovation was a planning process integrating the team's tasks and decisions. This was done over a six-week period spanning June and July, 1990. It was launched as a test of several new management techniques essential to implementing concurrency. Since there would be more than two hundred and fifteen DBTs constituted in a rapid ramp-up during subsequent months, what Section 41 pioneered would influence the methods that others would follow.

THE KEY PLAYERS

For Section 41 DBT, the new style really meant "two bosses with one hat." The team had two designated leaders, one from engineering with upstream team responsibility, and one from operations with downstream responsibility. The executive agreement to fuse Engineering and Operations empowered the **DBT leaders** with the influence necessary to integrate the activities of team specialists who would normally work sequentially.

For Section 41 the first **leader** was an experienced structures engineer. He came to the assignment without special leadership training or guidelines on how to manage a DBT. Luckily, a teaming facilitator assigned far more of his own time to help the leader. The **facilitator's** task was to outline a set of training procedures for planning and managing both the "concurrent" design process and the "digital" design procedures. Although excellent at his task, he too came to the assignment learning on the fly. Nothing existed in prior Boeing experience to describe the "how to" part of concurrent engineering. One of the facilitator's assignments was to design a handbook on procedures for the 777 under the title "Concurrent Product Definition (CPD)." Section 41 provided a testing ground for the CPD dos and don'ts.

A third key player was the **scheduler**. Traditionally his job is to make sure that a schedule for the full four-year process was created. This takes the form of basic GANTT charts that became progressively more detailed and complex the closer to final assembly they got. They become cumbersome wall-sized documents. Schedulers usually start by constructing a work breakdown structure (WBS), schedule each work element in it, and deliver the schedule

CONCURRENT ENGINEERING

to a project manager for implementation. Section 41 would have to change the scheduling rules. Since no one had ever planned or experienced "concurrency" before, it was difficult to schedule anything in advance. This was an immediate source of tension. It ran against the instincts of schedulers who traditionally dictated deadlines. It did not take long for old habits to re-assert themselves on Section 41 as the scheduling pressure took precedence over the need to carefully plan the total design process.

GETTING TO WORK

A trial exercise had been carried out with a few members of Section 41 prior to its formal launching. At that time 28 individuals were identified as the necessary value-adding team members. When the DBT pilot officially started, the number had been successfully reduced to a more manageable size of 14. The first trial planning effort showed three independent team "chimneys": engineering, operations, and support. The next iteration treated them as coequals under the generalized organizational heading of engineering/operations. It reflected an important organizational change and political agreements in the sharing of authority by senior executives. This, of course, reduced the team complexity.

The initial six weeks was set aside to develop a Section 41 work plan using a four-fields mapping process as an experimental format for the team's collaborative efforts and deliverables. An off-site location was chosen for the team to meet, only a block from the main engineering site for Section 41.

During the initial week, full work days were devoted to the planning. In the next two weeks only half days. Subsequent meetings covering an additional four-week period were held periodically at Boeing facilities in a special room arranged as a "Section 41 Control Center." Project documents and four-fields diagrams for each phase lined the walls. A new software program was introduced to the team as a shortcut to recording and drafting the four-fields maps (see Figures 11-3a and 11-3b). Although designed for eventual use as a networked tool accessible to all team members, it was used here only to edit process maps quickly. The team itself worked with adhesive paper flags and a 20-foot wall to lay out four years of work.

Figure 11-3a
The team at work

Figure 11-3b   Computer corner

This method allowed all members to communicate freely with each other about information on the wall. When a flow of tasks was agreed upon, the details were recorded on the computer by a support staff person. Printouts were ready by the start-up of the following session. Another novelty was the team's agreement to make scheduling secondary to a good definition of work process. This would give the members far more flexibility in juggling tasks and relationships than they would have if they were bounded by predetermined time and sequence constraints. The scheduler volunteered that this approach had produced the "best planning he had ever seen at Boeing." Despite this, his old scheduling biases set in shortly thereafter.

The team set out to work. None had experienced a collaborative effort of this sort in which tasks would be integrated and consensus between specialized engineering disciplines reached on a design process. Only a few had been exposed to the 3-D digital design protocols. All were surprisingly open to experimenting with a new five-step form of process mapping recommended by the consultant to the group and the facilitator:

1. Establish **master phases** following the overall project guidelines and deadlines.

2. Define preliminary **exit criteria** for each phase. Determining exit criteria was viewed as necessary before the team tried to tackle entry criteria at a later date.

3. Identify all **individual tasks** necessary to complete a phase without initially concentrating on linkages or concurrency between the tasks.

4. Reorder the tasks to show **downstream involvement** early in the design process and to establish **horizontal concurrency**.

5. Insert formal activities such as **meeting and reviews** that would enhance the quality of communication across the team and reduce design error.

6. Agree to common **terminology**.

The sixth item was added early in the process of discussing phasing. The team discovered significant differences in the language used by different disciplines to describe the "degree" of completion of a design drawing. This might at one extreme be a rough schematic and at the other a detailed drawing of a part. Adding to the confusion was that the 3-D system allowed the "degrees of development" to cover a wider span of detail. What was degree-one detail to one person was degree-two detail to someone from another discipline. It was just the kind of problem that Phil Condit, the 777 division chief, described as contributing to a costly process of design error and rework companywide.

One of the early achievements of the Section 41 DBT was an agreement on ten degrees of design detail. These were translated into common terminology, and each degree was illustrated with a drawing. Degree zero might be a simple stick-shaped drawing known as a centerline, Degree nine, a part design in complete detail. This proved to be a communication breakthrough that allowed all the disciplines to share a common frame of reference. Later, this allowed them to more quickly reach consensus on phase exit criteria.

Discussion over **phasing** proved far more difficult and time consuming than anticipated. It became evident that the full 777 master plan phase names and milestones, which a master scheduler devised, did not conform to Section 41's needs or terminology. After two days of extended discussion and debate, a ten-stage process was mapped out. It still met the needs of the master plan but included additional milestones. Exit criteria were then written and collected from each of the DBT disciplines and unified into a single set for each phase.

The evolution of the group's subsequent process mapping can be seen by comparing two iterations of a four-fields map for one of the phases. The first part of Stage Four was selected for reproduction here with task names edited out. Five symbols were used by the team to map the process (see Figure 11-4).

A comparison of two segments of four-fields maps produced one day apart shows the fine-tuning that comes from intrateam communication (see Figure 11-5). The first example simply shows sequential tasks that belong to each discipline. At this point in Section 41's planning exercise there is no effort to show horizontal linkages.

The second example shows two significant changes. The tasks are rearranged by the team so that concurrency of activities,

CONCURRENT ENGINEERING

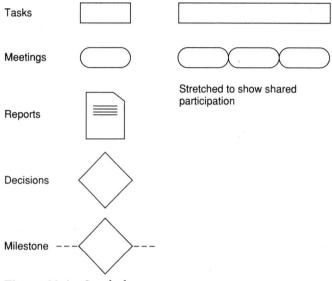

Figure 11-4 Symbols

parallel, in a logical flow, is highlighted. The other is the insertion of two integrative design review meetings attended by *all* team members—including downstream ones. Both these steps were innovations in the engineering design process at Boeing.

Under normal planning circumstances, the schedule would not allow time for a planning exercise like this to take place. The scheduler would simply work from a Work Breakdown Structure describing single tasks much as the first template above indicates. The scheduler, in addition, would be unlikely to worry about who from downstream should appear at an early design review meeting. Yet, it is just such qualitative aspects of cross-function management that allow the process to be streamlined and performance to be significantly improved.

Old-styled scheduling methods and critical path [PERT] analyses are more appropriate to processes, such as assembly, that have quantifiable constraints, for example, a machine-tooling operation of 12 seconds or a curing of a material for 36 minutes. Such characteristics lend themselves to finding a critical path that can be made no shorter or less costly. The same procedure has absolutely no relevance early in a design process because good

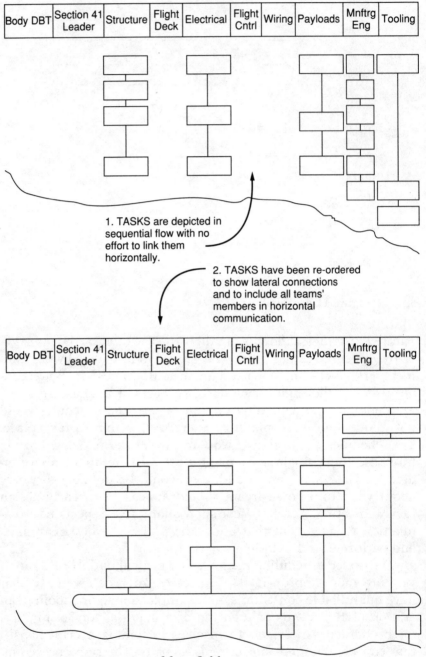

Figure 11-5 Fine-tuning of four-fields maps

decisions have less of a relationship to time or money than to how well team members communicate—a subjective criterion.

The preplanning work completed by Section 41 focused on process, not design, concepts. The purpose was to eliminate redundancies, encourage horizontal linkages, and bring downstream players in. Further effort by the team was required to link standards, design tools, and test methods to each of the mapped tasks and design reviews.

The results of Section 41's piloting work were substantial. Both procedures and methods for managing "concurrent" and "digital" design were altered and improved. A uniform design language was developed. And through its work Section 41 confirmed the validity of mapping the process in such a way that key features—such as exit criteria—are perceived as valuable design-control techniques. Above all, however, the initial Section 41 pilot underscored the value of intense and early communication between all team members.

The principal shortcoming, schedulers driving the process, has already been described. Others were more trivial but interesting. One example stands out. Software that supported the drafting of "four-fields" maps was adamantly criticized by a manager for not showing time lines flowing from left to right. Mentally programmed by GANTT charts to see time lines going from left (START) to right (END), he simply did not want to read a document in which time started at the top and moved downward. Like a Westerner unable to think of reading a book backwards, as Arab or traditional Japanese books are written, he had no interest in a printed document that did not conform to his mental preconception.

Section 41 illustrates the very beginning of a learning curve occurring at Boeing. In an ideal context, four-fields process maps, such as the one developed by Section 41, would be reviewed by a higher-level core DBT. This core team would not only review but also progressively improve generic teaming methods as it accumulated more and more examples of process maps from other DBTs. To be effective this ongoing review should be done by senior line people with direct responsibilities and not by staff remote from day-to-day operations. In this manner, process improvements are internalized by line people rather than "parked" in a corporate staff office.

This Boeing story confirms the payoff from opening lines of communication between team members. More importantly, the Section 41 experience, a microcosm of a far larger process, plants a stake in the ground demarking the end of an era of "management by silo." Replacing it is the integration of specialized knowledge through cross-function teams, or DBTs as Boeing labeled them.

Section 41's process improvements were a result both of a conviction that there was a better way—and of senior management willingness to experiment and let the team stumble by trial and error into a best method. What management provided was a "777" DBT support staff that was quick to learn on the job. The Section 41 experience helped it to produce Concurrent Product Definition training materials for subsequent teams.

It can be done. Change even in complex, entrenched cultures is possible. The payoff at Boeing will be measured several years downstream not only by delivering a new "customer preferred" aircraft to its clients but also by progressively taking advantage of the opportunity to eliminate enormously costly design error and rework during the plane's long lifespan. Cross-function process management, or what Boeing has chosen to call Concurrent Product Definition, aimed at breaking a tradition of compartmentalized silos is central to the challenge.

Notes

Chapter 11

1. *Aviation Week & Space Technology,* June 3, 1991.

12: SKUNK WORKS

T he TMEP[*] is an educational program cosponsored by two functional chimneys, manufacturing and engineering, at Digital Equipment Corporation. Formally known as the Technical Management and Education Program, TMEP's mission, in part, is to develop courseware for its technical managerial staff, two tiers down from the top-level management. One component of a four-part program introduces both the concept and practice of cross-function management. Its inclusion was an act of faith by the TMEP director and staff: Cross-function methods would meet an internal need at DEC for better process management. No one

* Insights and judgements on the activities of the TMEP are the opinion of the author based on his experiences as a cross-function teaming consultant to DEC. These views are not represented as those of DEC.

was clamoring for it. To succeed, cross-function training course-ware would have to find an audience and work its way into the corporate culture from the bottom up.

This story focuses on the cross-function course module and the role it played in gradually introducing change into a large, dif-fuse corporate culture. Because local managers could voluntarily select the program without higher-level approval, a decision to undergo the training and to apply it to a real project was akin to a skunk works. Risks in applying new methods could be taken "off the books." Success could be carried a step up for executive's approval and a formal sanction of the process.

Instituted in the spring of 1989, the TMEP fast-tracked itself into being a supplier of courses to engineering and manufacturing organizations worldwide. It addressed middle-tier managers with an offering of classroom case studies and blue-chip academics and experts. For the first-level managers, a tier below, the focus was on improving management skills on-the-job with their project teams. Four modules were offered to any first-tier group worldwide want-ing to voluntarily sign up.

DEC has in excess of 100,000 employees spread across the globe, a third of them in an agglomeration of locations in Massa-chusetts and southern New Hampshire. A fleet of company-owned helicopters ferries among them. The headquarters are called "The Mill" because the original 19th-century buildings were home to an enormous textile mill situated along a water source for power. Cheap rents and later a cheap acquisition price brought Ken-neth Olsen, the company founder and president, here. In the early days of the company, computers were assembled inside pressur-ized tents to prevent the dust-laden ceilings from disrupting the electronics.

Out of this environment was crafted a product strategy con-sisting of small computers arrayed in a distributed system. Mini- and microcomputer hardware linked together with efficient net-working technology became the Digital imprint. The concept ran against the basic foundation of IBM's mainframe view of comput-ing. This strategy worked, but also helped blindside the company. It never managed to enter the PC or the desktop market as a lead player. That side of the market fell to Silicon Valley vendors and the IBM PC. Internally DEC was managed as a vertically inte-grated firm supplying much of its own componentry.

Digital promotes individual entrepreneurship as a corporate style. Ad hoc teaming is the modus operandi. Meetings are a primary mechanism for communication and problem solving. Meetings follow meetings. If you have an idea, you lobby, gather a team of supporters, meet, and lobby for further support. This approach has a self-selecting magic to it. If the idea is good, people will flock to it. If the leader is good, the same will happen. If both are off key, no one will.

"To get people thinking about what's important," wrote *Fortune* magazine, "Olsen solicits proposals from DEC's lower echelons and tosses out thoughts of his own. 'Ken is always flying ideas around the company,' says William Long, a former vice president. 'Sometimes they're like little paper airplanes aimed at a particular person; sometimes they're like leaflets from the Goodyear blimp, aimed at anyone who picks them up."[1]

The problem is that while this method of management breeds creativity, it can also generate enormous inefficiency. No one has computed the dollar or time cost of this "invisible" entrepreneurship, but one clue is in the "unrecorded" time spent lobbying for an idea. For example, no one wants to come forward for approval until both the idea is proven and the team is on board. Under standard corporate guidelines, all this would be considered "prec-oncept" planning, or what Digital formally terms Phase 0 Planning, but it is actually done before Phase 0. This not only makes it *invisible* to corporate leaders and departmental budgets, but it absorbs valuable energy away from ongoing projects. Many efforts may actually be counterproductive by working at cross-purposes or by being redundant. As a result, when actual development cycles for a project are measured, Day One of Phase 0 is usually many months after the actual start-up occurred. This conceals the real amount of time spent. It allows a lot of fudging by project managers who will push start-ups as far forward as possible in order to "look good" in meeting tight deadlines.

By the 1990s, a two-tiered system had developed at DEC. This meant, in a highly simplified form, that at the top a corporate team initiates strategies and coordination of the enterprise globally. However, the top operated more and more through institutionalized chimneys representing both vertical functions like research, sales, service, and manufacturing, and three major sales regions, which were: North America, Europe, and the rest of the world. At the bottom, multitudes of teams struggled for recognition, resources, and executive support. This was definitely not a GM-styled command-and-control company, nor a bullish newcomer like Sun Microsystems.

For DEC, a clear avenue for improvement lay in tightening horizontal links between teams, vertical function chimneys, and regional chimneys. But because no senior executive or committee had that cross-company responsibility, there was no formal process in place by which to achieve it. The cross-function TMEP skunk works was an experiment in developing a more disciplined companywide process management at DEC.

THE NEW KID ON THE BLOCK

The cross-function module, managed and marketed within DEC, consisted of a two-day course, a train-the-trainer component, and a self-paced videotape with segments linked to each of eight course components. The content was a simple step-by-step introduction to four-fields mapping techniques. Each step required that course participants reflect critically on the company's current practices. Three "process" maxims were used as a framework for this self-analysis:

First maxim: Maximize the Opportunity for Human Interaction (e.g., eliminate organizational and other barriers). Participants were asked to reflect on the hurdles inhibiting companywide human interaction such as administrative requirements or narrow reward systems.

Second maxim: Minimize Waste (e.g., strip out non-value-adding activities). How much effort is expended doing work that has no direct bearing on the intended result?

Third maxim: Respond to Customer Needs (e.g., define process requirements up-front). How effective is the company in gauging customer requirements and producing effective results that meet those requirements?

Teams exposed to the module generally concluded that Digital spoke of itself as a cross-function company but actually operated as a vertically managed firm. In other words, an informal culture worked across boundaries, while formal systems worked at cross-purposes by imposing organizational boundaries. An example would be a rewards system encouraging sales representatives to meet short-term volume targets while systems integration teams worked on long-term solutions with a client. Another might be a teaming effort to sell a global networking solution to a Fortune 500 company but a fragmented geographical sales and service structure with no financial incentive to sell "global solutions."

Within an 18-month period about 30 teams took the course. They represented diverse groups, from semiconductors to distributed systems, from Singapore to Massachusetts to England. Reaction and results ran from high enthusiasm and commitment to lukewarm feelings depending, in part, on a team's enthusiasm, the quality of trainers, and the need cross-function methods seemed to fill.

On the positive side was the role four-fields mapping played in getting project team members to buy in to a whole process and not just narrow tasks within it. "For the first time it lets us see the whole project from beginning to end," reported one team leader. "It's an excellent way to make a presentation of a program to a senior manager. It integrates all the program elements neatly and well." Perhaps the single most appreciated aspect of the training sessions was that "it gets us to talk together as teams."

The first blush of enthusiasm by many teams was tempered by the chore of drafting four-fields maps. Doing them by hand the one time was accepted as a part of the training exercise. Drafting and redrafting them by hand as an ongoing activity was seen as a waste of time. A software support tool, they suggested, would not only facilitate but also proliferate continued interest, especially given the ubiquity of terminals at DEC. This need stimulated Digital to make support software available onto its own VMS/Ultrix computer system. This gave internal teams the tool, the network access, and the data management capability to offer four-fields mapping as an easily accessible corporate resource.

THE CMOS TEAM

One example of a TMEP skunk-works effort in cross-function management was a nine-person team within the Semiconductor

Group developing a new CMOS (metal oxide semiconductor). After a concentrated effort coached by the TMEP module coordinator, Marsha Greenberg, her enthusiasm being a key to the propagation of the methods, the CMOS team developed a 10-month preimplementation process map. At the end of their training, they listed the advantages and disadvantages of using the four-fields cross-function approach.

- The concentration on getting parallel versus sequential effort saves time.

- Errors and disconnects are discovered far earlier.

- It greatly improves the "buy-in" and the efficiency of the hand-offs.

- By developing a road map, everyone can see and reference what is happening.

- It led us to share technical resources, whereas otherwise each group would have had to have expertise in every area.

- Communication is now coordinated.

- It developed a strong commitment to the final outcome.

On the disadvantage side, four items were identified:

- The total process appears longer to each group member due to the change in how they are involved: Each member is coming in at day one versus coming in at day 400.

- Increased communication takes time.

- Technical experts may have difficulty sharing technical decision making as time goes on.

- Cross-functional management is not the norm and people may lack skills in how to do it.

Pinpointing downstream needs such that problems could be anticipated and averted was considered a significant plus. This allowed the team to plan for an improved test chip strategy, a qualification strategy and the needs it would meet, clearer advance packaging requirements and evaluation methods, and standards for judging success along the way. They added new decision points, coordinated feedback loops, and clarified communication needs across the team. Although they all agreed to work independently, they planned to regroup at scheduled times to sort data, reach consensus on critical points, and plan revisions. The key to getting this to happen, they agreed, was a strong program manager empowered to lead the group from the start.

In the particular product category the team focused on, a study of a competitor's latest product development indicated that it had shaved three months off its schedule and turned a product out in 18 months. In addition, it had managed to produce a better product with only 49 integrated circuits as opposed to 640 in the prior version. Even screws in assembly had been reduced dramatically. This benchmarking provided a horizon against which to target or measure their own achievements. The team's conclusion of the TMEP training, made in a report to senior managers, was curt. "The time to start is now."

THE PHANTOM GROUP

A different problem was tackled by another team within the telecommunications and networking group known as TNN. A manager signed up for the cross-function course with a clear problem in mind. He wanted to bridge a serious communication gap between hardware and software engineers. To do this he gathered a 14-person team from various engineering disciplines to diagnose why the TNN group experienced product-development problems. He called the effort "Project Phantom" with a goal of "recommending changes to the product-development process to improve: time-to-market, predictability, the work environment, and the ability to meet customer requirements." An in-house project was used as a guinea pig. The four-fields method was used to dissect the project's principal strengths and weaknesses.

Several problems were isolated. Vision, it was determined, was not well communicated from the top of the corporation down. This created confusion in the team's view by making key product trade-offs difficult. Leadership was seen as a problem because of conflicting loyalties to the project and the organization chimney to which individuals belonged. In addition, the company's reward system was seen as working at cross-purposes with the project requirements. This was exacerbated by a lack of useful metrics to apply to the project team's overall performance. A lack of "process" management training for project managers was seen as an added problem.

For each of these problem areas specific cross-function process recommendations were outlined. These were later taken to the TNN group's senior vice president. Persuaded that this was a management methodology worth pursuing, he delegated a staff person as an advocate of the team's recommendations. This led to the creation of a new cross-function program aimed at reducing time-to-market.

This example illustrates the movement upward of a successful skunk-works effort in process management. Through the steadfast commitment of the manager who had first enrolled in the TMEP course and his ability to inspire the involvement of the full Phantom Project team, behaviors among the team members and ultimately the group's senior executive were affected. Significant, too, was the ability of the TMEP program to offer strong trainer support in understanding and using cross-function process tools and techniques.

These efforts have created interest by word of mouth. Late in 1991, a team in another divisional group decided to make the cross-function project management methodology the basis of a new product development project. Supported by two trainers, external consulting services, and access to newly available cross-functional project software, its leader and his core project members committed to an extensive front-end planning process using the four-fields framework to stimulate communication between each of the disciplines.

Several lessons learned stand out from the TMEP training experiences over a period of about two years. One is that the quality and commitment of the trainers is an essential ingredient in carrying the message of new cross-function methods. Because Marsha Greenberg and a staff colleague, Carlene Merrill, gained both a mastery over the subject and a strong conviction in its importance to DEC, they were able to act as its "missionaries." In cases in which the trainers were equipped with only a cursory introduction to the methods and had no particular commitment to the concept of cross-function management, the training process failed to provide value to participating teams.

Another lesson is that the personal interest of a manager wishing to apply cross function—or skunk work—methods in an actual project is critical. That person must be ready to learn the techniques and commit himself or herself to them. Without the leader's hands-on knowledge of process management techniques, team interest is harder to sustain and the risk involved in experimenting with new methods is heightened.

TOYOTA/BOEING/DIGITAL...

The three cases illustrate significantly different attempts to break silo-like management structures. In Digital's case, a culture of individualists recognized that a more disciplined teaming process could actually enhance their individual talents by getting to their common goals faster and better. At Boeing, the recognition was perhaps more political than cultural. The barriers were at the top. Once broken there, as they were by getting Engineering and Operations to join hands, the team players below mirrored the signals from the top. Political agreement can be costly, as a senior executive told the author. "I've used up all my political collateral to win this one for the 777, don't come to me with anything that requires another ounce of political will. Just do what you have to do to change behavior with Section 41 but don't touch the organizational structure."

Boeing and Digital are just two American examples. Others have been hard at it for even longer periods. Ford's Lewis Veraldi pioneered cross-function teaming with the Taurus project. His successes were institutionalized under the Concept-to-Customer and subsequent World Class Timing programs. But despite considerable effort, Ford still has not broken thick barriers separating functions and departments even after ten years of trying. It is a high-stakes battle. It puts careers, perquisites, reputations, and personal insecurities to the test.

SKUNK WORKS

Hewlett-Packard, Kodak, and Hughes are part of the tip of an iceberg of firms willing to experiment with new management methods; many of these firms point to horizontal linkage as the most difficult bridge to cross. What is becoming evident, too, is that there are more ways than one to skin a cat. Part of the experiment in finding new ways to arrive at the same end lies in the American penchant to experiment with computer-driven solutions. This is explored in Part IV: Electronic Tools.

Notes

Chapter 12

1. "America's Most Successful Entrepreneur," *Fortune*, October 27, 1986, p. 27.

PART IV

ELECTRONIC TOOLS

The concept of work itself changes in the electronic age. The effectiveness of the office worker originates in his ability to deal with many variables simultaneously, to probe for new answers that were not previously accessible.

Paul A. Strassman [*The Information Payoff*, The Free Press, NY, 1985, p. 127.]

New organizational units [may] develop which could not have grown through conventional media, encouraging group creativity and consideration of radical alternatives that might otherwise have been identified or considered, or easing the pains of matrix management by providing a forum to resolve cross-organizational conflicts.

Bob Johansen, et al. [*Leading Business Teams,* Institute for the Future, Addison-Wesley, 1991, p. 89.]

13: THE CHALLENGE

Access to companywide information is vital to the effectiveness of TQM management. Access is often extended to include suppliers and customers who are treated as members of cross-function process teams. For these reasons, electronic tools are an essential backdrop to getting information to the right people at the right time, particularly if they are geographically dispersed. But while increased electronic storage, processing speed, and communication capabilities provide solutions, they are also exacerbating the need for accessibility by causing data accumulation rates to increase exponentially. Paradoxically, electronic enterprise integration could also be the beginning of an information nightmare rather than an electronic solution.

There are 60,000,000 desktop computers in the United States. A typical new laptop computer can hold 20 megabytes of data on a hard disk no larger than a couple of cigarette packs. While this represents a memory capacity several orders of magnitude higher than just a few years earlier, it is not enough. My own 40-megabyte computer is filled with "simple" word-processing software applications that take up larger and larger chunks of memory. For a design engineer, a single typical computer-aided drawing may require 1 to 2 megabytes. This drawing, in turn, may be only one of 30 to 1,000 other drawings comprising a product design. To manage this complexity new workstations are needed with 50 to 1,200 megabytes of memory and access to even more storage through "servers." This example easily suggests the enormity of the data explosion. The workstation may allow the designers to solve more complex problems, but in the process it creates massive new data-bases.

In many cases, the information-sharing process has reached extremes that are less and less manageable. A study prepared by Digital Equipment Corporation of a big-three automotive company found that "one model year ultimately resulted in over eight million separate sheets of paper." (See Figure 13-1). The same report concluded that "most organizations are still in situations where the 'high tech' tools used by engineers to create and analyze designs, are accompanied by 'low-tech' technology to distribute and manage this data and information."[1]

THE DREAM...

Several "what ifs" would fulfill the dream of a seamless data management system.

- What if I were able to simply "point" on a computer screen to the location of the latest version of files or documents stored somewhere in a network, and click? This is currently impossible in a world of incompatible equipment and software standards, organizational impediments, and regulations prohibiting access to certain files.

- What if I could have direct, on-line, network access to files and documents stored on computers?

- What if I could ensure access control and safety? Nobody wants to create a system that has no way of monitoring who enters and exits or who edits files.

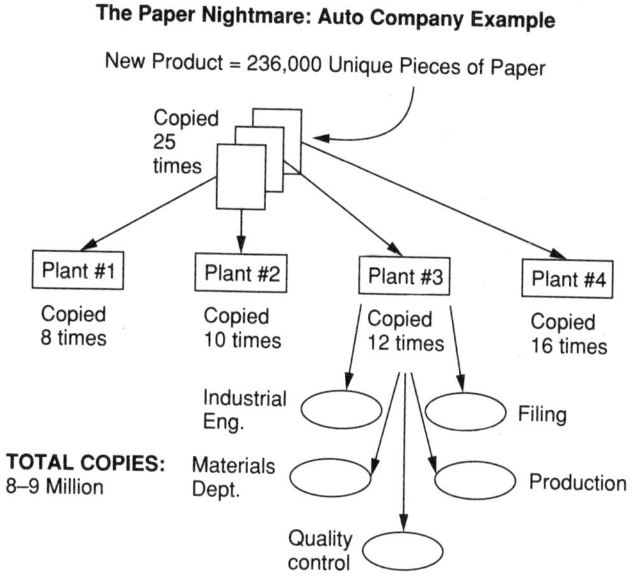

THE CHALLENGE

The Paper Nightmare: Auto Company Example

New Product = 236,000 Unique Pieces of Paper

Figure 13-1

- What if I could have a "meta record" automatically created that would show me document histories with dates of changes, who did them and why, and content summaries?

- And, what if I could have a way of doing configuration management, meaning the ordering of all this documentation and information into logical hierarchical groupings according to the type of product or process being managed?

This wish list describes an easily accessible information-sharing system that is essential for companywide teams to operate effectively. If the team is managing a full product life cycle, this means marketeers, designers, engineers, manufacturing personnel, logistics specialists, sales, service, finance, and corporate office sharing a common data base. The numbers of players involved can grow into the thousands.

SOLUTIONS

Solutions to the wish list start with the appropriate management model. If the model is hierarchical and fragmented

THE SEAMLESS ENTERPRISE

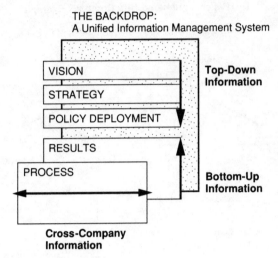

Figure 13-2   The TQM model and
information management

into functional silos, the information systems will only mirror the organizational structure. This is why TQM and cross-function process management are so important as the framework for building electronic tools. It provides a holistic overview of a total process and the work elements contained in it (see Figure 13-2). Departmental barriers are either secondary or nonexistent. The cross-function four-fields process map, like a conventional road map showing a list of town or street names with a grid reference, allows appropriate data and documents to be tagged to the appropriate task as a common resource. This makes the location of relevant data sources accessible to all team members. If the map were on a computer screen, it would bring us closer to the "what if I could just point to the data I needed." This is explored in the chapter entitled "The Control Panel."

All this begs for real-time solutions that collect and disseminate data simultaneously to "all who need to know." Just as an automated airplane reservation systems responds to information fed to it in real time, for example, seat availability is presented as of that instant and a booking is automatically inserted and instantly seen by all other agents, the same is increasingly true of business. Data captured at a supermarket checkout counter by a laser beam is instantly fed into a corporate information system.

THE CHALLENGE

Each additional bit of data is accessible to an analyst in real time. He can adjust inventories, direct certain items to be discounted, and adjust the positioning of other items on shelves based on real-time information. Similarly, data on defects, sales, inventories, warranty complaints, or competitive products is strategically important to a company. *Everyone* should know, *not just a narrowly specialized chimney.* Shared awareness of the same information—in real time—allows a design engineer to react from one perspective, a sales representative from another, and a financial officer from a third. This process, akin to parallel processing in a computer, leads an organization to react in a patterned or holistic manner, as a team rather than in a fragmented, sequential fashion.

Kao Industries, a major Japanese competitor of Procter & Gamble, makes use of its 50,000 employees as real-time data gatherers on product tests, competitive evaluations, and user feedback. The raw data that they gather is widely distributed as strategically valuable information necessary for Kao to constantly adjust product ideas, distribution methods, and pricing. The company thinks of each employee, and his or her family and friends, as an antenna able to feed information back.

For Boeing Commercial, a major innovation of the 777 project management process is its real-time digital designing process that allows engineering designs to be developed and corrected by teams in real time. The system creates, in addition, an opportunity for "virtual" access to the inventory of the airplane's 3,000,000 discrete parts by anyone of several thousand designers and future maintenance technicians. Managers of the 777 estimate that they will save 18 months over conventional methods in getting engineering design ready for assembly because of this on-line feature.

French-created CATIA software, used to manage the digital design, is "really a communications tool," says Larry Olsen, director of the 777 airplane team's computing systems. "The crux of the new design process is to bring the various parties together up front, and the tool for doing this is CATIA."[2] Everyone has immediate access to the same drawing from the very beginning and through subsequent changes. Two thousand workstations are linked together through the CATIA system.

THE SEAMLESS ENTERPRISE

Another part of the solution is being driven by the Department of Defense. The Computer-Aided Acquisition Logistics Support (CALS) program initiative, a big-bucks development project, is moving into a second phase calling for the creation of something that in ubiquitous Washington acronym-ese is called CITIS: Contractor Integrated Technical Information System. It requires that all contractors, subcontractors, and the DoD entities involved in a specific program have access to the same data by electronic means. The purpose of all this technology is to gain control over the "process." The aim is to reduce both inefficiency and waste because the old system is literally sinking from its paper weight.

Interestingly, another example of electronic tools to support seamless communication is ABC's Ted Koppel's "Nightline" TV program. It is a visionary form of electronic conferencing; it can put millions of people into two-way contact either through five or six intermediaries appearing side-by-side on a split screen or through marathon group discussions, as Koppel did one night in an auditorium half full of Palestinians and half full of Israelis, or as Peter Jennings did when he linked U.S. audiences live to query Gorbachev and Yeltsin in Moscow. Within companies, teleconferencing, electronic bulletin boards, notification systems, and mail services are now common.

Some companies, such as Digital or Toshiba in Japan are completely networked with most of their employees reachable through their terminals. More than 90,000 employees are "addressable" at DEC allowing electronic conversations to be carried out through interactive "Notesfiles," a product used internally and sold to many of the company's clients. A subject category can be opened and addressed to as few or as many employees as desired. The note accumulates comments, ideas, give-and-take debate, and facts. People can open the notefile and read or comment on it at their leisure. Three thousand different subject files can be accessed within the company. This tool has brought enormous value to Digital by making its global network of employees and information sources as accessible as possible. The medium is used as much to resolve complex technical issues as it is to share practical tips on restaurants and hotels in cities worldwide. One of its hidden strengths is that it allows the option of making comments anonymously. An employee can criticize a colleague or superior without fear of retribution. "If this were done as video conferencing," said an employee, "we'd be right back to old-style power plays. Having video wouldn't really add much value." (What if employees were allowed to rank the performance of superiors anonymously over a network?)

Pressure for "virtual" environments is driven by the new rules of competition: customer-driven markets, continuous improvement, and concurrency. Each feeds on making information available as it happens. If a customer complains, the full product team should know immediately. If a problem happens, the company wants to get to the cause and a systemic solution right away. If concurrency is to be effective, it is by making information accessible to all players simultaneously.

But in many cases, networked operations aggravate the problem. At Ford Motor it was a surprise to the engineering design department to find that computer systems sold as "cost-savers" were in fact expensive "cost creators." No one had anticipated the cost of making it easy to make design changes. Every change required updated worldwide information databases, revised manuals on parts and service, and altered training materials. Increased design flexibility, in this case, was a more expensive solution, not an easier and cheaper one. Cases such as this are additional arguments for instituting more disciplined process management. The problem does not look simpler as we get nearer to the year 2,000.

Product data management systems (PDMSs) are one component of the solution. A PDMS is akin to a supramanager of all files, data, and documents that are created or used during the life cycle of a product such as the Boeing 777 or a simple motor for a windshield wiper on a car. The data is broad based. It may include customer requirements, quality characteristics and specifications, project plans, business plans, manufacturing process plans, designs, test data, performance data, regulations, standards, schedules, and budgets. From a TQM cross-function point of view, all this data and documentation "belongs" to a companywide knowledge team rather than being segmented into parts owned by a dozen or more departments reluctant or unable to share or to distribute their information. PDM Systems outlines the architecture of companywide information management necessary to support cross-function teams. The important point, however, is that no

---

THE SEARCH IS ON

In some ways the EDM [Electronic Data Management] problem parallels what happened when computer automation first appeared on the shop floor. Certain points in the production process were automated, but little or no attention was given to how these point solutions should be integrated with the rest of the production process.... Because it crosses departmental boundaries, success will require the emotional buy-in of engineers and designers as well as commitment from the top....

An EDM solution shouldn't be pursued until the engineering data flow is clearly identified and charted.

[EDM: The Next Step Toward CIM, *Industry Week,* 2/5/90.]

---

information system will work if applied to the wrong management model.

Yet even with the right model, the dream of electronically integrated enterprises—a missing piece to crafting the seamless enterprise—could remain an elusive often Sisyphean challenge. However, a new form of teaming "collaboratories" and the creation of information system "control panels" offer innovative insights to the making of seamless enterprises.

Notes

Chapter 13

1. "Product Data and Document Management," by the Engineering Systems Group, Digital (Munich, Germany), 1988, p. 9–10.
2. *Aviation Week & Space Technology,* June 3, 1991, p. 50.

14: COLLABORATORIES

When Toyota and Komatsu conceived "cross" functions, a true management breakthrough was engineered. The next breakthrough is coming with a new generation of electronic tools becoming known as groupware. These tools present American firms with the first genuine opportunity to translate cross-function practices into a powerful teaming concept.

Companies and universities have been experimenting with groupware for more than thirty years. Xerox's Silicon Valley laboratory pioneered various forms of simultaneous electronic interactions starting in the early 1960s. Project Athena is a more recent effort launched by MIT in the early 1980s with the unusual combination of IBM and DEC teamed up as sponsors. MIT was chasing an ambitious goal. It wanted to develop software that could allow an individual to tap into several computers and run several programs simultaneously through windows adjacent to one another on a single terminal screen. The goal was achieved with a solution it termed "X-Windows." It is now a standard available to most buyers of sophisticated workstations.

But more importantly, MIT's Athena project and others like it were setting the stage for an even more important idea, the idea of many people working together in "virtual" simultaneity from different locations. The American Heritage dictionary explains *virtual* to mean: "Existing in essence or effect though not in actual fact, form, or name." This ambition is being fueled by the rapid maturation of desktop computers such as Macintosh that provide a cheap and friendly user interface and a new generation of software designed to serve groups.

VIDEO WINDOWS

Employees of Bell Communications Research, Inc., who wander into the snack room at a research center in Morristown, N.J., casually trade grins, waves and suggestions with their counterparts in Navesink, N.J., even though Navesink is 50 miles away.... The 8-foot high Video Windows that virtually bring these distant groups into the same room at the same time are a product of a new technology intended to expand drastically the amount of data that optical fibers can carry.

"The electro-optical bottleneck is how fast we can turn lasers on and off," Professor Acampora said. The limit is 1 billion to 2 billion flashes, or bits of information, a second; fiber can carry at least 500 billion bits.... Video Window's [developed by Bellcore] two optical cable links carry 45 billion each by compressing signals.

Eric J. Addeo, a research manager...described the Video Window as an attempt to create "virtual presence"—the feeling that the person on the screen is really on the other side of the table. "With a near life-size image and high quality audio, there is a sense of naturalness that is not present in typical teleconferencing," he said.

["Adding Lanes to Data Highways," *The New York Times*, 7/24/91, p. D19.]

FROM VIRTUAL LABS
TO COLLABORATORIES

The term *collaboratory*, first used by the Institute for the Future at an April 1991 conference in Mountain View, California, means *shared experience* and *shared learning* supported by electronic *groupware* technologies. This creates a uniquely American concept of "virtual" cross-function knowledge teams: teams that can communicate and function even if they are geographically distributed. This expansion of the original Japanese notion of companywide teams has far-reaching implications given a Western bias toward individualism and a Western liking for electronic tools as communication devices. Strangers are happy to converse electronically in ways that are considered both alien and uncomfortable to Japanese.

A "collaboratory" is an electronically supported knowledge team operating in four possible situations: people working at the same time in the same location; people working at the same time in different locations; people working in different locations at different times or people working at different times in the same location. (See Figure 14-1). Electronic technology plays a central role in making information available to groups in each of these four collaboratory situations.

This vision of "virtual group intelligence" provides structure to an emerging generation of groupware technologies. "The basic groupware building blocks are the telephone, the computer, and

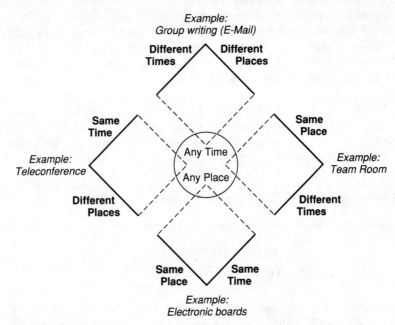

Figure 14-1 Collaboratory classifications (Source: Adapted from the Institute for the Future)

the conference room," states the Institute for the Future. "Almost all groupware tools and applications build on this infrastructure." Cost, speed, and value-adding through increased intrateam contact, data sharing, and communication are principle benefits of using these tools.

Concurrent engineering is a *collaboratory* groupware concept. Its tools are already familiar: CAD, CAE, CAM, CIM, or CIE [similar tools exist for software]. At one extreme (Computer Aided Design), the tools are limited to specific disciplines; at the other extreme (Computer Integrated Engineering) the tools are designed to link diverse disciplines, corporate departments, and suppliers together. The DoD's CITIS (Contractor Integrated Technical Information System) fits into this category. The goal is to press for simultaneity in the design and manufacturability of products and thereby eliminate waste.

COLLABORATORY GROUPWARE DESIGN TOOLS:

CAD   Computer Aided Design
  CAE   Computer Aided Engineering
    CAM   Computer Aided Manufacturing
      CIM   Computer Integrated Manufacturing
        CIE   Computer Integrated Engineering
             or Computer Integrated Enterprise

"Design for manufacturability," which is the simultaneous electronic development of design concepts along with the necessary manufacturing techniques, involves groupware technology. It is computer- and telecommunication-dependent. Product designs are conceived on computers in such a way that manufacturers can design the necessary production tools while taking production requirements into consideration. This eliminates making drawings, building handmade models, and designing tools in sequential, time-consuming tasks.

At the same time, a host of new competitively priced nonengineering collaboratory applications is entering the market. Software, such as Aspects, that allows dispersed teams to edit documents simultaneously and interactively, is an example. Of the same genre are automated meeting schedulers that will access individuals' electronic schedules and determine optimal times for a team to meet.

Current groupware technologies are not without their short-comings. Data does not always travel easily between computers made by competing vendors. More applications need to be developed that take group needs into account. And telecommunications methods are still far from sophisticated when it comes to creating virtual voice, image, and data proximity between geographically dispersed groups. Among the innovators, however, is the Microelectronics Center of North Carolina. A semiconductor research center founded in 1979, it linked six academic centers together so that engineers, faculty, and students could interact in "real time" in solving problems by voice and by sharing data even though they were distributed at sites as far as 175 miles apart. The voice and data system was oversubscribed the day it was put into service.

Some of the concepts and technologies associated with collaboratories go back to Doug Englebart, the inventor of the computer "mouse," who stimulated the first experiments with groupware technologies at the Augmentation Research Center at Stanford Research Institute, in 1967. A cartoon building on ideas that evolved from these early experiments shows a person saying: "It allows

---

SEEDS PLANTED IN 1960s...

Doug Englebart's [group] in the late 1960s and early 1970s had capabilities within each of the four time/place cells. For same time/same place, Englebart had a team room where the moderator had a full workstation and each of the participants had a mouse. Several monitors were recessed within the circle of tables around which everyone sat. For *different time/different place,* there were shared journals and group writing capabilities; screen sharing, audio links, and even motion video on a split screen were available for the *same time/different place.* Finally *same place/different time* capabilities were in place.... so that team members could use the center at any time of the day or the night—even if other team members were not present simultaneously.

[*Leading Business Teams,* Bob Johansen, et al., Institute for the Future, Addison Wesley, 1991, p.20.]

different time, different place, different personalities, we call it groupware." Another person in the cartoon responds by saying: "In California we call it channeling."

IBM has created its own network of "decision conference center rooms." At last count 30 existed with sophisticated communications and workstations supporting teams of 10 to 15 people. An estimated two-thousand work sessions have been carried out in these rooms over the past few years. Other companies, such as Xerox, have pioneered similar environments. But until recently the technical cost has been too high to make it a cost-effective process. In addition, innovators have puzzled the question of what best uses of collaboratories might be. What problems can be best solved through the medium of collaboratories?

Cross-function process management is ideally suited. Since it requires close coordination and communication companywide, it is tailor-made for collaboratories. The concept of process *control panels* introduced in the next chapter may be instrumental in facilitating the introduction of cross-function teaming.

15: THE CONTROL PANEL

Many complex activities are managed through a control panel. In an electrical utility plant, a control panel consists of numerous gauges, sensor lights, and flow controls. In an airplane a similar array of instruments provides the pilots with real-time information on equipment functions, hydraulic systems, flight paths, or cabin temperatures. These panels are all designed to manage "process," or HOW things are happening rather than the result. The electrical utility control panel looks at the making and movement of electrons—not the result of delivering them to someone. The airplane cockpit controls tell the pilot HOW the airplane is behaving and only by extrapolation about the result, where and when the plane will land.

Applying the same control panel analogy in business, the manager has few if any ways of looking at a total cross-function process and judging HOW well it is doing. Even with the best current methods, coordination and communication is difficult. J.P. van

Overveen, a senior mechanical engineer at BART (Bay Area Rapid Transit), describes the U.S. state-of-the-art in railroad and transit engineering management in 1990. "Nearly every physical and engineering discipline is involved in a design effort and yet the various efforts are loosely coordinated, if at all. There appears to be little communication between those responsible for the civil works, architectural effort, and track construction on the one hand, and those responsible for the design, construction, and operation of the vehicles on the other side. Certainly an effort is made but it is haphazard and there is no concerted effort to tie the project together."

Tracks and vehicles—if mismatched—will quickly wear each other out. A heavy track will gradually destroy a light vehicle; a heavy vehicle will demolish a light track. Van Overveen suggests: "The vehicle design parameters such as weight, speed, steel profile, wheel diameter, truck design, ratio of sprung to unsprung mass should be more closely coordinated with the track design and the signal and communication design.... Otherwise much learning time [and cost] will be wasted."[1] Van Overveen first penned these ideas in the early 1970s. During the intervening twenty years *nothing* had changed; no fundamental improvements to the engineering process had been introduced in his view.

The cross-function four-fields method, as a software tool, is the first true control panel allowing a manager to monitor a more complete process. As a process design tool it maps team "plays," for example, combinations of tasks, meetings, and reviews, or the HOW TO DO IT. It provides electronic access to the "rule book," or corporate standards, governing all these activities. What Japanese managers never intended, and still have not perceived, is *the utility of the four-fields map as the format for an electronic process control panel through which to manage data seamlessly.*

Because the cross-function four-fields map describes a whole process, all relevant information such as documents, data, test method, and design review guidelines, can be tagged with the network address. One click of the mouse and any stored document can be seen on a terminal screen: profiles of cross-function team members, the activities that they will engage in, reports, meeting records, and designs they generate, schedules, budget records of actual and predicted expenditures or revenues, or results of a test. The four-fields control panel not only provides a picture of a whole process but access to the data and documentation behind it.

A "view" into all this documentation is achieved in two ways. One is by opening "windows" that layer different levels of information onto the screen, one on top of the other or side by side. Another view extracts data from anywhere in a network. Since almost any data has a reference code (a number or numbers and letters or a name), it carries an address, and it should be readable. Documents can be linked by address to any activity on a four-fields map. Only one original of a map need exist—not multiple copies reproduced electronically or on paper.

In this fashion any "knowledge team" can map a process, identify all the documentation pertinent to' it by address, and share the "control panel" over a network as a common resource with all team members. This provides the whole team, whether it consists of a few or numerous members, with a common point of reference and data accessibility. Without such a control panel, team members are left to their own ad hoc measures. Such ad hoc teaming does not contribute to the total corporate learning process because it is not recorded in a uniform and easily retrievable manner.

A simple contextual diagram of how a process "control panel" might function looks like this (see Figure 15-1).

A virtual cross-function product development collaboratory at work might proceed as follows. A new product development

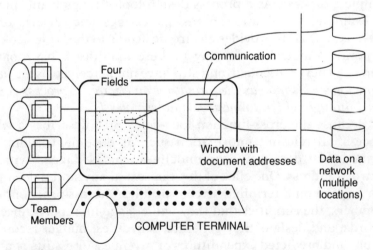

Figure 15-1 Looking at the total process: The networked cross-function team

team is called together to plan a 14-month development schedule for a new workstation. Three of eight key core team players show up. Five are dispersed thousands of miles apart. The team leader has set up a simple "same time different place" collaboratory. All eight core team members are hooked up by speaker phones. In addition, a simple network has been established with one computer in the meeting room linked to each of the other member's terminals in their offices. An inexpensive new device projects the screen image to wall size. Windows allow anyone to edit or manipulate information in any chosen window. What one person does on-screen is seen by everyone else.

The first meeting includes an initial mapping of the four-fields process and a discussion of preliminary product concepts. To set the stage the team leader has roughed out the skeleton of a four-fields diagram and faxed it in advance to everyone with some handwritten notations on information each needs to bring to the meeting. The meeting has progressed for about an hour and the four-fields process map is now on-screen.

Leader: "It's important that we focus on the first preconcept planning stage. Last time, everyone landed on us for not getting good input from Marketing up-front."

Marketing: "Don't blame me, you guys got started before I even knew that you had a new idea in mind. Remember when I finally plugged in, you guys had forgotten that our customers were yelling and screaming about the delays from the connector cables you forgot to plan for. They want cables that give them far more flexibility."

Leader: "OK, what do you think? How about our first tasks being to pin down our initial product concepts ... Let's label the next task 'Get customer information.' Who wants to be involved?"

Marketing quickly inserted two or three additional tasks on the four-fields map. Other team members interjected ways in which they could add information and insight into those tasks.

Engineering: "Wait a minute. I'm going to get the specs on the last project in a window. Maybe we could use them as a starting point." A prior project four-fields map was called up and the specs document clicked open. "Look, there's a lot there we can re-use."

The team narrowed the list to four critical elements it would need customer input on. In a separate window, Marketing wrote up the list and sketched out a number of questions it would pursue with customers. Engineering and Service each added a couple more.

Marketing: "Can you guys look into some of these questions? Maybe we should be gathering a better profile of the competitors' products?"

By the end of the day, an intensive exchange of ideas had occurred. All eight members felt better connected to the project, its goals, and ways in which they could contribute to one another's success. The communication had been fluid, and useful information had been captured on-screen in real time. Documents were called up from the network and reviewed by the group, also in real time. The value added, in retrospect, was enormous. For the first time, this team felt that it had gotten a handle on the front end of its development process.

The key to this extension of cross-function knowledge teaming is that by merging the concept of process control maps as an electronic interface and integrated data management system, the user, for example, any team member, is a mouse click away from any data resource. The complex and sophisticated technology linking him or her to the source should be absolutely invisible.

Software that was used to draft some of the four-fields examples in this book, is one of a first generation of cross-function process management tools. These first-generation tools provide a process control panel interface, windowing capability, and ease of retrieving data sources from a network. The next tools of the generation will be simple, easy-to-use-data management tools that work transparently across the different vendor computers, networks, and software.

Each companywide cross function represents a corporate knowledge team with a large information base underlying it. This includes user surveys, regulations, Quality Tables, design schematics, parts descriptions, customer files, and any number of other documents. By using a four-fields mapping as a control panel showing a whole beginning-to-end teaming activity, the process and relevant data and information can be made uniformly accessible across company boundaries. It is a resource necessary to achieving the integrated or seamless enterprise.

Notes

Chapter 15

1. J. P. van Overveen, "Railway Engineering: A Systems Approach?," Unpublished Paper, Bay Area Rapid Transit (BART), Oakland, California, 1990.

PART V
CHANGE

America faces a problem that is simply put. The huge Technological edge enjoyed by Americans in the 1950s and 1960s has disappeared. Whereas America once had effortless superiority, it is now faced with competitors who have matched its economic achievements and may be in the process of moving ahead of it. If present trends continue, America's standard of living will fall relative to those of the world's new industrial leaders, and it will simply become another country—Egypt, Greece, Rome, Portugal, Spain, England—that once led the world economically but no longer does.

Lester Thurow, MIT, *Zero-Sum Society*, 1985

16: FIRST STEPS

There is nothing simple or easy in a decision to change a management style. Tomes and tomes have been written about how to do it and how not to. In many cases what is missing in the literature and counsel on "change" is a clear vision of a management style inspiring the directions of change. This book offers an insight into a new style of management. Its principal feature is an innovative cross-function process that is compelling competitive response to the three new rules of competition: customer-driven quality, continuous improvement, and task concurrency.

Instituting the new style can be achieved in all varieties of ways. However, two clearly different options stand out. One starts at the top with a recognition by senior executives that *process management* will be important to the firm as a competitive strategy. The second starts at the bottom. Authorized or unauthorized skunk works are often initiated out of frustration with ineffective formal corporate systems. Cross-functioning methods are ideally suited for skunk-work piloting aimed at breaking silo-like systems. The DEC "TMEP" story is an example. Successful skunk-work efforts, usually kept alive by an individual with a deep commitment to process improvement, will gradually wind their way up the corporate ladder and eventually capture the attention of senior managers.

However, for change to be institutionalized, the interest and commitment of senior management is a *sine qua non*, from the CEO down. This commitment must include three pre-conditions if change is to be successfully implemented.

■ *Senior executives or managers who institute a program* must **train themselves** *in cross function process methods before they delegate a follow-up. They must be committed for the long haul.* Leadership by example is compelling. Xerox's Roland Magnin, speaking at the first Malcom Baldrige Forum in Hartford, Connecticut, offered this insight as a key to his company's quality success. "We insist that the process start at the top and that senior people themselves learn enough to be able to train those working for them." This means that executives should be willing to invest the time necessary for the effects of cross-function procedures and methods to become apparent. Effective training itself will take a long time to cascade down to the middle-level ranks where change is often hardest to institute. Leaders with short time horizons and an impatience for immediate results are not ready for cross-function process management.

■ *A corporate* **core team** *must be responsible for monitoring and reviewing the implementation of cross-function management methods.* The temptation of a CEO is to assign process changes to a staff function with responsibility both for implementation and monitoring. This kind of delegation not only meets resistance from senior operational people who are reluctant followers of staff initiatives, but it generally removes them from both influencing and designing process improvements. The involvement of line people is also critical in achieving a political buy-in to major process improvements. The core team functions as the company's eyes and ears on process improvement strategy. Without it the CEO is in the dark on what works, what does not, and what improvements might affect the company's competitive future.

- *Individuals selected to pilot or implement a cross-function process must be* **empowered** *with budgets, authority, and the option to fail.* When it comes time for the CEO and the core team to delegate implementation of process improvements, those doing it must feel fully empowered to make judgments, allocate resources, and call for appropriate actions when necessary. This empowerment will not come easily because it runs against entrenched work habits built around rewards and against careers structured around vertical chimneys. This aspect was acknowledged by Boeing Commercial's 777 teams as the reason for failure to institute process changes in the aborted 7J7 project that preceded the 777. The latter was launched only after a major political agreement was reached between the Engineering and Operations chimneys to act as a single development unit and not as two arms-length chimneys. This decision made it easier to empower Design Build Team (DBT) leaders. This process did not always work as smoothly as anticipated because of entrenched habits by engineers used to functioning within narrowly specialized boundaries.

If these preconditions are met, several steps follow.

Step One: Assess the opportunity

The first step in adopting cross-function management methods is to **assess** the scale of the process improvement opportunities. The trigger for an assessment is often a "we've got our backs to the wall" competitive situation. This is the kind of pressure that Ford felt in 1980, that Wang laboratories felt in 1988, and that Goodyear Tire felt in 1990. The message is simple: improve the way you manage or go out of business. When I first started to visit Ford plants in the early 1980s, it was common to find production lines with 30 percent of the product being scrapped or reworked. GM, in nationally circulated ads lauding its quality improvements, admitted to overall defect rates running at 800 per 100 cars in first year of use. It is now down to 140 but still 30% worse than the best. AT&T, soon after its break-up, was alarmed to find itself losing seven out of ten bids for large-exchange systems. The reason was a bureaucratic process that took months too long to craft a proposal and often did it without taking client needs fully into account.

Such findings can be alarming. A recent case at a large computer firm revealed that complicated administrative procedures involved in managing a "sale" cost the company more than it earned. It cost about $8,000 to administer a sale. This meant that a client ordering a single $500 item would result in a net loss to the company of $7,500. It took about five years for this company to realize that its new chief financial officer was doing more harm than good with the auditing procedures he instituted.

The core team's "opportunity" assessment is concluded by listing and prioritizing categories of improvement. This is what, in fact, led Japanese innovators such as Toyota and Komatsu, to discover the three key proprieties for process improvement: *quality* (meaning meeting customer requirements or lowering warranty costs), *cost,* and *delivery* (meaning quantity, time, and packaging). The product development cycle is the most evident context for corporate teams to focus process improvements on. This, indeed, is what Hewlett Packard with its Product Generation Teams, Boeing with its Concurrent Product Definition, or Ford with its World Timing process, have chosen to do.

Step Two: Appoint a process core team

A formal assessment is best carried out by a cross-function knowledge team appointed by the CEO or Divisional Vice-president. This **core team** represents various divisional or chimney responsibilities. The team might also choose to benchmark its corporate operations against a best-in-class target value. This will allow it to target a value, such as the "half-lives" instituted by Analog Devices and a timetable within which to do it.

	Actual	Best	Target
Project development cycle	60 months	40	50
Defect rates	6/100 units	1/u	2/u
	150 parts/million	3 ppm	5 ppm
Design error/rework	3 reiterations	1 time	1.5

FIRST STEPS

What is significant about the analysis is that the opportunities for improvement—or what I have called the 30 percent factor—are everywhere. Look for them and you will find them. What is equally significant is that cashing in on them is a result of *process* improvement and not necessarily a result of costly equipment purchases, new buildings, or extra staff. *This is why cross- function management holds such great opportunity for American firms.* The payoff is enormous. That this is not fanciful is evidenced in the results of TQM efforts introduced by more and more companies. Some examples illustrate the point.

Marlow Industries is a 150-employee company with annual sales of $13 million. It produces small thermoelectric coolers for fighter jets and fiber-optic networks. Demanding clients in Japan pushed the firm to initiate a TQM program in 1987. By 1991, the results more than demonstrated the 30 percent opportunity.

- A 56 percent increase in productivity per employee since 1987

- An 18 percent increase in world market share since 1988

- A 47 percent decrease in costs involved with product failure since 1989

- A 320 percent increase in production capacity since 1989.

As the corporate core team's and other cross-function teams' experience increases, a broader set of priorities can be addressed such as personnel training, purchasing, or information management. These are more subtle and perhaps more difficult to coordinate because the results of improvement lend themselves less to precise measurement.

Step 3: Target a pilot project

Once the process priority is established, do not waste time planning the "perfect" follow-up. The best method is to go out and do it in "real time." Results will come if a pilot effort is selected with a short enough time fuse to show results. A *product-development process* with a manageable idea, budget, and time frame is a fitting pilot project. Four to six months is a good test. A few superior people on a pilot team will more than overcome the absence of a "perfect" formula for change. They will invent and improvise.

Cross-function methods and techniques can be tested and improved, and lessons can be learned for dissemination to subsequent teams. It is important that the pilot be "visible." By having a high profile, it signals the importance of the experiment to other parts of a company. This visibility means that a pilot project should be selected such that the odds of success are high. This will generally be ensured by assigning dedicated and competent people to work on it who are empowered to make decisions as they see fit. This is in great part the lesson of Section 41 at Boeing. It served as a high-visibility pilot, testing methods and techniques that other Design Build Teams on the 777 would later emulate. Because Section 41 is the most important single component of the aircraft, its selection as a pilot project added political and emotional significance. It was the "real thing."

Step 4: Use the cross-function "toolkit"

The cross-function management toolkit is just what it says: a set of generic methods that can be applied to a variety of situations and needs. One of its distinguishing characteristics is that it is not an arbitrary top-down management dictate: "there is only one way to do it." Quite to the contrary, the toolkit, if properly used by managers, is a mechanism for coalescing all the energies of all employees in a firm. Its purpose is to allow *managers and employees* to collaborate in mapping its own companywide process. This empowerment taps a deep well of latent energy.

Summarized in a simple graphic format introduced in earlier chapters, the toolkit builds on an underlying organizational structure consisting of vertical "silos" or "chimneys" with responsibility to produce results. Running laterally across is a cross-function team made up of line representatives from each chimney. That team, as the graphic below summarizes, has a set of tools and techniques available to it (see Figure 16-1).

The pilot team has five basic tools and techniques to use: four-fields mapping, Quality Function Deployment (QFD) procedures, design reviews, hierarchical methods of analysis, and an organizational structure that runs horizontally across the firm. Computer

FIRST STEPS

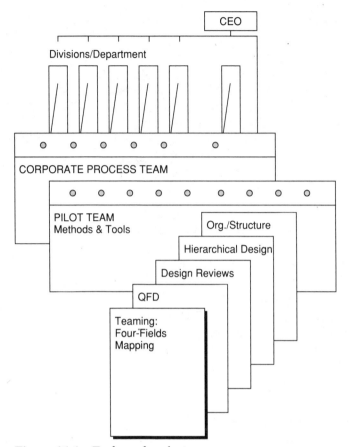

Figure 16-1 Tools and techniques

and communication networks will play a role depending on the sophistication of the pilot. At Boeing they were crucial given the decision to plan the aircraft electronically on 3-D systems. On far smaller projects, such as DuPont Electronics connector team, colocation of an eight-person team was reinforced by networking their workstations together.

The novelty of this approach is that the team is given a toolkit that puts the emphasis on process. "Let's decide how we can work together and map it out to meet all of our needs," is another way of phrasing it. Whenever the author has introduced this approach to new teams, their reactions have always been the same. "It is just terrific to be able to work out all needs together in advance.

We've never done it before. This way we all know what is expected and we've played a role in deciding how each one of us best fits into the total project."

This empowerment running laterally across a company is the key to the successful introduction of cross-function techniques. It not only unleashes new energy and commitment, but it induces a different innovative thought process. Because different people are together in a room from the start, the logic, shared ideas, and the solutions are more holistic and comprehensive. The process works every time, at all levels of a company.

Step 5: Review the pilot

The core team can monitor the ongoing work of a pilot. At minimum, it should review the full pilot effort in order to judge the effectiveness of the cross-function toolkit. This will lead to improvements in tools and techniques, additions of more subtle refinements, and the possibility of developing company-specific training materials on cross-function practices. This is the first commitment by the core team to building a generic description of the process and an actual "case." It is the first level of knowledge developed by the core team in cross-function process management.

Step 6: Plan and implement a rollout

Based on the lessons learned from the pilot, the core team can either choose to end the experiment or to plan a wider rollout across other product-development teams or across other cross-functions such as purchasing, cost control, and other company-wide issues.

Conclusion

The executive holds the TQM cards. The TQM will or will not work based on his or her understanding and belief in its concepts and benefits. To make it work, however, the executive must have the competencies to lead the quality process. Therein lies a dilemma. For many executives there is considerable confusion and uncertainty about quality practices. This makes it hard to take risks, to delegate responsibilities, or to empower others. It is far easier under such circumstances to resist or postpone change.

FIRST STEPS

Cross-function management is one of those uncertainties. It means many different things to many different people. It sounds hard and time-consuming. To some it means teams of people from other chimneys over which an executive may have little direct control. It means playing a game for which there may be no direct reward or recognition on a performance rating. And worse, it may mean sticking one's neck out over other people's turf. In the political arena of executive corridors this can be a kiss of death.

This book was written to help lift some of the confusion or uncertainty about what is meant by cross-function management. At the same time, it was written with the purpose of introducing a framework of tools and techniques that might be of immediate use to a senior executive or a risk-taker willing to skunk a project. In either case, a well-executed effort will yield an enormous return.

The impact of cross-function empowerment was driven home to me a long time ago during a visit to a Ford automotive plant at the suggestion of Louis Veraldi. During a conversation with several assembly line workers in a small coffee room, one of them looked at me and said: "You know something, there's a collective genius out there on the shop floor. They just didn't know how to take advantage of it."

If this book has been helpful to the reader, my hope is that it is for one single reason: that it provides a key to unleashing that collective genius in American enterprises.

APPENDICES

QUOTATIONS

Several items are included that provide lengthier quotations on *cross-function management, quality management,* and *scientific management* from individuals mentioned in the text. These include (with dates of origin of the material):

- **Kozo Koura**, Lecturer, Aoyama University (1990)
- **W. Edwards Deming** (1951)
- **Frederick Winslow Taylor** (1911)

A more detailed explanation of *concurrent engineering* and *computer-aided acquisition and logistic support* (CALS) follows from the:

- **Institute for Defense Analyses** (1988)
- **CALS/CE Industry Streering Group** (1991)

ON CROSS-FUNCTION MANAGEMENT

by Kozo Koura, Lecturer, Aoyama Gakuin University [Unpublished manuscript, 1990]

*T**he main effects of the introduction of cross-function management are given by Kozo Koura as follows:*

1. The decision making by cross-function concepts such as quality assurance, cost and profit control, production and delivery control, etc., can be done quickly and all company operations can be carried out smoothly and to better effect.
2. The significance of cross-function management is thoroughly diffused throughout the company, communication between divisions, coordination between divisions, and personal relationships are improved.
3. Problems are studied by cross-function and the increase in new vertical departments and sections can be kept to a minimum.
4. It becomes easier for the strata below division chief to make proposals to their superiors.
5. Executives become much better managers. They stop being concerned merely with profit of their own divisions, and

become more flexible as their horizons expand to include the company as a whole. They become more open to mutual co-operation and support....

More on Corporate Cross-Function Teams

1. The team has real power. Its decision making capacity concerning business and operational affairs should be very near the top.
2. Team members should only be executives. There is no need to include all specialists and members of related divisions. Deliberations should be carried out in the same manner.
3. The cross-function team is created flexibly (establishing temporary coalition functional teams, enlarged functional teams, project teams, working groups, etc.)
4. It is easy for members to get into the habit of promoting the welfare of their own divisions, but it is necessary for them to broaden their horizons to include the entire company, and not to confuse cross-function topics for discussion with cross division conversation.

STATISTICAL TECHNIQUES IN INDUSTRY AS A NATIONAL RESOURCE (1951)

By W. Edwards Deming (Bureau of the Budget, Washington, D.C.) [Speech to the Bureau of Industrial Statistics, Calcutta, India]

It is necessary that the quality of products be expressible in terms that the buyer and seller understand. Price without knowledge of quality in intelligible terms is meaningless. Moreover, quality is meaningless except without reference to the consumer's demands. Statistical methods not only help to produce uniform and dependable quality: they provide also a world language in which to express quality and in which to conduct negotiations, even though buyer and seller are in different parts of the globe....

We must remember that terms such as good quality and desirable uniformity have no meaning except with reference to the consumer's needs and his ability to pay. It follows that statistical quality control is the application of statistical principles and techniques to all stages of production, directed toward the most

THE SEAMLESS ENTERPRISE

economic manufacturing of a product that is maximally useful and has a market....

Turn for a moment to the problems of coordination. The purchasing department, design department, the production department, the inspection department, and the consumer relations department must all deal daily with standardization and tests. Each of these departments, left to itself, devises its own standards and tests, which are too often found to are in annoying conflict, and of unequal or even doubtful validity. Thus, uncoordinated, a single department, through the techniques that it uses, will frequently commit other departments and the entire company to some policy that brings trouble to management later on.

THE PRINCIPLES OF SCIENTIFIC MANAGEMENT (1911)

by Frederick Winslow Taylor [Reprinted in Scientific Management, by F. W. Taylor, Harper & Brothers Publishers, New York, 1947, p. 39]

Perhaps the most prominent single element in modern scientific management is the task idea. The work of every workman is fully planned out by the management at least one day in advance, and each man receives in most cases complete written instructions, describing in detail the task which he is to accomplish, as well as the means to be used in doing the work. And the work planned in advance in this way constitutes a task which is to be solved, as explained above, not by the workman alone, but in almost all cases by the joint effort of the workman and the management. This task specifies not only what is to be done but how it is to be done and the exact time allowed for doing it. And whenever the workman succeeds in doing his task right, and within the limit specified, he receives an addition of from 30 percent to 100 percent to his ordinary wages. These tasks are carefully planned, so that both good and careful work are called for in their performance, but it should be distinctly understood that in no case is the workman called upon to work at a pace which would be injurious to his health. The task is always so regulated that the man who is well suited to his job will thrive while working at this rate during a long term of years and grow happier and more prosperous, instead of being overworked. Scientific management consists very largely in preparing for and carrying out these tasks.

THE ROLE OF CONCURRENT ENGINEERING IN WEAPONS ACQUISITION (1988)

by Robert Winner, James P. Pennell, Harold E. Bertrand, Marko M. G. Slusarczuk [Institute for Defense Analyses, IDA Report R-338]

The following is excerpted from the full report of the IDA:

Definition

Participants at the first IDA concurrent engineering workshop discussed concurrent engineering practices in several U.S. companies. They described the use of methods that included traditional system engineering practices and new engineering and management approaches. DoD and Air Force initiatives to improve the acquisition process were also presented. Based on the discussion at that workshop, on further contributions from participants, and consultation with various reviewers, the following definition was developed:

Concurrent engineering is a systematic approach to the integrated, concurrent design of products and their related processes, including manufacture and support. This approach is intended to cause the developers, from the outset, to consider all elements of the product life cycle from conception through disposal, including quality, cost, schedule, and user requirements.

Concurrent engineering is characterized by focus on the customer's requirements and priorities, a conviction that quality is the result of improving a process, and a philosophy that improvement of the processes of design, production, and support are never-ending responsibilities of the entire enterprise. The philosophy of concurrent engineering is not new. The terms "system engineering," "simultaneous engineering," and "producibility engineering" have been used to describe similar approaches. In fact, a number of authors have described similar techniques and hundreds of companies have applied them successfully. Nevertheless, many companies have *not* adopted concurrent engineering because of the "fundamental, wrenching, far-reaching transformations that are required throughout the enterprise."

The integrated, concurrent design of the product and processes is the key to concurrent engineering.... In the sequential method, information flows are intended to be in one direction. In the concurrent approach, information flows are bi-directional and decisions are based on consideration of downstream as well as upstream inputs. The companies studied in this report found that achieving this sharing of information required both organizational and technological change.

Where changes were made, concern for *survival* in the face of increased competition, particularly from Japanese manufacturers, often provided a new incentive for companies to improve the quality of their products and increase the efficiency of their product development processes. As the pressure to improve quality and efficiency increased, new computer-based design and analysis tools gave specialists from different engineering disciplines the freedom of working with the same description of the design to evaluate the effects of particular design features. The companies that have been successful in concurrent engineering have embraced the philosophy of continuing improvement, and they are using new tools as well as traditional techniques to implement this business philosophy.

Although the study team found examples of companies that are moving in the direction of concurrent engineering, none of them claimed to have developed "the one best way." The people affected by the changes say that progress has been difficult, that mistakes have been made, and that enthusiastic advocacy and support by top management have been essential. None of the companies said that concurrent engineering, in isolation, is capable of producing the type of improvements needed to remain competitive. Concurrent engineering is part of an integrated corporate competitiveness plan. Nevertheless, they are pleased with their accomplishments and they are actively looking for additional improvements.

Classification of Activities

The study team identified three complementary classes of activities among the initiatives described:

1. engineering-process initiatives such as the formation of multidisciplined teams;

2. computer-based support initiatives such as improvement of computer-based design tools, including giving the user an environment that integrates separately developed software; and

3. use of formal methods including application of special purpose tools for design and production support.

The first class of actions are initiated by management and seem to be the first elements implemented. There are cultural barriers to these initiatives, but with management support they can be overcome. Getting an integrated computer-based support environment is a difficult technical challenge. Developing a culture that takes continual advantage of observation and problem solving to create knowledge is a never-ending challenge. The three classes of initiatives are discussed in greater detail below.

Engineering process initiatives are management actions to improve the organization and the procedures used to develop a product. Leadership at the highest corporate and government levels driving continuous quality and productivity improvement is a prerequisite for successful implementation of concurrent engineering. Changes to the status quo, especially the cultural changes required for concurrent engineering, are not likely to be successful or to endure without top management leadership and support.

Early involvement of representatives of manufacturing is a minimal step in this direction. Most of the case studies show that companies form teams which include marketing, production, engineering, support, purchasing, and other specialists. Team members are selected for their ability to contribute to the design effort by early identification of potential problems and by timely initiation of actions to avoid bottlenecks. This is not equivalent to forming committees where members often delay decision making; instead design teams get faster action through early identification and solution of problems. In some cases, the effectiveness of design teams can be traced to recent advances in management disciplines and information system developments. Most of the companies visited during this study have undertaken substantial education efforts in this area. Other management initiatives include the following:

- emphasizing attention to customer needs and quality improvement,

- improving horizontal integration of the organization,

- promoting employee involvement in generating new ideas for improvement,

- requiring engineering comparisons of proposed products and competitive offerings, and

- establishing closer relationships with suppliers to include supplier involvement during conceptual design.

Computer-based support initiatives cover a range of computer-aided tools, database systems, special purpose computer systems that improve design verification, and computer-based support of product design, production planning, and production. The companies differ in the sophistication of their systems, but those companies making advances in this area share a goal of using a single data object as a source for many engineering functions including design synthesis and verification as well as planning production processes. This use of a shared, common data object by specialists throughout an enterprise provides a mechanism for concurrently performing the product and process design tasks.

A solid model of the object being designed is frequently used as the single data object that allows automated systems to be integrated. In many cases, several companies comprising a development team are sharing access to the same solid model. Among companies doing electronic design, simulation is a critical tool. Mechanical design, tooling, machining, and assembly need accurate solid models. Feature-based design and group technology are approaches to creating and imposing regularity on the design process.

Aircraft companies use finite elements models (FEM) and computational fluid dynamics (CFD) to support design. In attempting to provide rule-based design systems, several companies are developing practical applications of expert systems.

Formal methods are difficult to categorize. This class includes process control techniques that date to the 1930s, such as statistical process control (SPC), design of experiments, newer tools (such as design-for-assembly developed by Boothroyd Dewhurst Inc.), and a range of quality engineering techniques for managing complex system trade-offs and for finding optimum design and production process parameters. These include statistical tools for data analysis such as design-of-experiment, robust engineering principles as proposed by Taguchi, quality function deployment (QFD), and the techniques used by Pugh. Other methods that have been useful in problem solving include Ishikawa's seven tools, response surface methods, group technology, exploratory data analysis, and fault-tree analysis. These methods are used for different purposes, but they are all designed to help people understand the behavior of processes, products, mechanisms, and so forth, which otherwise could not be understood as thoroughly. If used properly, the methods and tools are a tremendous aid in design, production, and engineering, yielding sharply reduced life cycle costs, shortened design cycles, and improved quality.

The apparent diversity of the formal methods sometimes masks the more important process that takes place when they are used properly. This underlying process is the scientific approach to problem solving. For a company to be successful using the approach, its employees must develop the habit of identifying problems and solving them so as to improve the company's processes. Once problems are identified and analyzed, the choice of a particular formal method will depend on the situation.

An SPC standard was developed for the War Department in December 1940 by the American Standards Association. It is a technique for using statistical sampling methods to determine the regularity of a process. The original standard was revised and the use of SPC is described in ANSI Z1.1-1985, Z1.2-1985, & Z1.3-1985.

Design of experiments or experimental design was invented and developed in England in the 1920s by Fisher. It has been used in agriculture, medicine, and biology. In manufacturing, design of experiments provides tools for designing and conducting experiments in an efficient way so that optimum values for product and process parameters can be identified. Deere and Company reported using traditional methods for design of experiments.

Design-for-assembly software is commercially available to help designers evaluate the benefits of using fewer parts, better fasteners, and more efficient assembly techniques. One product was developed by Boothroyd Dewhurst, Inc. and has been licensed by approximately 300 companies in the United States and Europe. Many dramatic product improvements have been reported through its use, particularly in the automobile and consumer products industries. Ford Motor Company recently reported total savings in excess of $1 billion through widespread application of the Boothroyd Dewhurst software system.

Pugh is a proponent of encouraging creativity during the conceptual design stage and using unbiased evaluation criteria to develop the strongest concepts.

Robust design has come to be associated with Taguchi. His engineering innovations and statistical methods, however, can be addressed separately. He has introduced some new and very important quality engineering ideas. He stresses the importance of closeness-to-target rather than within-specification objectives. He recommends using statistical design to formulate a product or process that operates on target with the smallest variance, is insensitive to environmental disturbances and manufacturing variances, and has the lowest possible cost.

Robust design is achieved through system design, parameter design, and tolerance design. System design is a search for the best available technology, parameter design selects optimum levels for design parameters, and tolerance design establishes the manufacturing tolerances. Parameter design and tolerance design make use of planned experiments. Although there is general agreement that the principles of robust engineering are an important contribution, the question of the selection of statistical methods for conducting the experiments and analyzing the results remains open within the scientific community. The terms "Taguchi Experiments," "Taguchi Methods," and "Design of Experiments" are sometimes used interchangeably by practitioners. This report uses the terms that are applied by the person who performed the experiment.

Participants in the concurrent engineering workshops were clearly opposed to any initiative that imposes some rigid guideline for using one or more of the formal methods. They believe that each company should be free to decide which techniques are most useful in a particular situation. Moreover, one group of participants concluded that individual formal methods could be used independently of other methods.

Reported use of the methods varied considerably. Only three of the companies studied (AT&T, Aerojet Ordnance, and ITT) reported making extensive use of robust engineering and Quality Function Deployment (QFD). Boeing described an initiative to restructure their systems engineering process to perform many functions included in QFD. IBM described a top-down design method that sounded very similar to QFD.

This initial study does not include a survey of which methods are most widely used in the United States. A recent article from Japan describes the statistical methods mentioned in the presentation to the annual quality circle conference. The most widely used methods were the Ishikawa tools, design of experiment, and tree analysis (QFD). *Table 2* lists the frequency of use of various methods at the 1987 Japanese quality circles conference.

Misconceptions

There are misconceptions about concurrent engineering. To help overcome them, it is helpful to describe what concurrent engineering *is not*.

First, concurrent engineering is *not* a magic formula for success. The best system cannot compensate for a lack of talent. The companies studied have hired and trained engineers who are able

Frequency	Method
78	graph
43	design of experiment
40	Pareto chart
40	tree analysis & QFD
39	cause & effect diagram
36	histogram
22	scatter diagram
18	FTA
18	correlation & regression
13	control chart
10	ANOVA
10	computer techniques
9	statistical test & estimation
9	others
8	multiple regression
6	relation chart
4	FMEA
3	process capability
3	Weibull distribution
3	simulation
2	principal component analysis
2	discriminant & cluster analysis
2	quantification theory
1	time series

Figure A.T. 2-1

to identify important design parameters, and who are capable of creating solutions to problems. At least one of the companies said that a significant part of their success was the fact that people worked harder. Concurrent engineering is an approach for improving the efficiency of good people who work hard; it provides no guarantees of success.

Next, concurrent engineering is *not* the arbitrary elimination of a phase of the existing, sequential, feed-forward engineering process. For example, it is not the simple, but artificial, elimination of a test-and-fix phase or of full-scale engineering development. Concurrent engineering does not eliminate any engineering function. In concurrent engineering, all downstream processes are co-designed toward a more all-encompassing, cost-effective optimum design.

Next, concurrent engineering is *not* simultaneous or overlapped design and production. Concurrent engineering entails the simultaneous design of the product and of the downstream processes. It does not entail the simultaneous design of the product and the *execution* of the production process, that is, beginning high rate production of an item that has not completed its test, evaluation, and fix phase. That approach is very risky. On the contrary, concurrent engineering emphasizes completion of all design efforts prior to production initiation.

On a somewhat less dramatic, but equally important note, concurrent engineering is not just design for producibility, or design for reliability, or for maintainability. Concurrent engineering includes all of these with the added requirement that the objective is for the design optimization to integrate these domains within a cost-effective engineering process.

Also, concurrent engineering is *not* the same as conservative design. Conservative design seeks robustness by using derated parts, redundancy, extremely close tolerances, etc. Thus, both conservative design and concurrent engineering may entail robustness but by different approaches. In conservative design, higher cost parts, that is, those that are better than apparently required or those that are built to a very high tolerance, are routinely used to achieve high quality. In concurrent engineering, robustness is sought by attempting to optimize over a larger set of processes and by determining how to achieve the resulting target values with the lowest cost parts. The evidence found in this study shows that concurrent engineering does not necessarily lead to more conservative design. Instead, concurrent engineering leads to products being tolerant of use and manufacturing variation and at less cost than sequential design.

Concurrent engineering also does *not* imply conservatism with respect to the incorporation of new technologies in the product.

Finally, concurrent engineering does *not* require conservative testing strategy, a completely different approach to high quality. Here, conservative testing means a strategy in which robustness is achieved by *planned, repeated* test-and-fix cycles (refining the design through testing). Concurrent engineering tries to approach one-pass designs in place of repeated test-and-fix cycles.

Because concurrent engineering is dependent on a total quality management philosophy, skeptics sometimes confuse it (concurrent engineering) with a misapplication of quality improvement, conservative inspection. Concurrent engineering does not imply conservative inspection strategies. Instead, it seeks to achieve manufacturing repeatability through product robustness and by designing a manufacturing process that includes the means for monitoring and controlling itself (either manually or automatically). There was widespread acceptance among the workshop participants of the axiom that inspection alone does not improve quality, does not avoid problems, and does not improve profits. Conservative inspection strategies are necessary only in a few application domains and these can be identified early in advanced design. In the typical situation, concurrent engineering techniques seek to eliminate the need for conservative inspection. Test-and-fix cycles can be viewed as the conservative inspection strategy for engineering....

Critical Functions

With regard to the *timing*, there must be an early understanding of the needs of all customers (buyers and users) and the requirements of all phases of the life cycle. This is accomplished by having an open and active dialogue between customer and vendor. This dialogue would, over time, transform a fairly vague set of requirements into the best specific set of time/cost/performance values available at the time. Along with the evolution of the understanding of requirements, there must be an evolution of a verification procedure that will check the eventual product against the requirements.

The process must change to ensure an effective and timely contribution of all responsible participants in the design/manufacture/use cycle and the objective identification and evaluation of trade-offs. The design process must allow, encourage, in fact, assure that:

- all requirements of the life cycle are considered and evaluated,

- the cross-impact of various functional decisions are understood and evaluated (with appropriate trade-off analysis),

- critical risks of various design options are identified and addressed early in the process, and

- those responsible for the various functional areas within the development and manufacturing enterprise participate with appropriate levels of responsibility and authority.

To achieve these objectives, concurrent engineering suggests four specific functions. First, there must be an integrated and continuing participation of multifunction teams in the design of product, process and support. Second, this process of integrating multiple engineering and management functions must provide for efficient iteration and closure of product and process designs. Third, the system must identify conflicting requirements and support their resolution through an objective choice of options based upon a quantitative or qualitative comparison of trade-offs, as appropriate. Fourth, the concurrent engineering process must incorporate an optimization of the product and process design. [Note: the optimization here should not be interpreted as any theoretical optimum of any individual design objective, such as system performance (for example, aircraft speed), but a very best possible combination of the most desirable objectives as defined by the customer.] This optimization can be based on either empirical or analytical (theoretical) knowledge (or both).

The philosophy of the entire enterprise must be one of continuous and aggressive improvement against current and projected product and process baselines. This, in turn, leads to a change in corporate focus from one of reaction to problems, to one of problem prevention.

There are four specific functions which contribute to this continuous improvement. First, open and continuous communication is necessary. This communication links the customer and the vendor and it also unites the many specialists involved in developing, producing, deploying, and supporting a product. Second, a complete (necessary and sufficient) and unambiguous statement of the users' requirements must be developed, including the priorities of various requirements to be applied in the case of trade-off analysis. Third, a complete and unambiguous description of the product and related processes must be provided to allow concurrent engineering to occur. Fourth, a baseline product and process evaluation must be established.

These three functional area changes, timing, process, and philosophy, are elements which characterize concurrent engineering. They are the differences between concurrent engineering and "good engineering practice," as it is executed in the U.S. today. All three elements are essential and of equal priority.

CALS: BACKGROUND, OBJECTIVES, AND STRATEGY (1991)

by CALS/CE Industry Steering Group,
National Security Industrial Association

CALS: Background

The introduction of computer-aided engineering, computer-aided design, and computer-integrated manufacturing has led to the automation and integration of various forms of technical data. This has enabled process improvements in many companies which have contributed to improved flexibility, responsiveness, and quality while reducing costs. To develop complex products, companies are forming trading partnerships and using industrial networks for the digital interchange of technical data. Through this process, they have recognized the need for standards to achieve interoperability with dissimilar computer systems.

The Department of Defense recognizes that advanced computer technology and telecommunications capabilities can greatly reduce the lead times and costs associated with the acquisition and support of weapon systems while improving their quality. The paper flow between industry and DoD today includes massive volumes of technical data. Millions of engineering drawings and millions of pages of technical manuals are delivered each year. The transition from paper to the digital exchange of technical data has already begun, not only in defense, but in the commercial segments of our economy. DoD's plans for this transition are closely aligned with the broad trends that are emerging throughout the private sector.

Computer-aided Acquisition and Logistic Support (CALS), established by DoD in 1985, is a DoD/Industry strategy for the transition to automated interchange of technical data, and to the process improvements enabled by automation and integration. CALS focuses on the generation, access, management, maintenance, distribution and use of technical data associated with weapon systems such as engineering drawings, product definition and logistic support analysis data. In 1988, the Deputy Secretary of Defense directed that steps be taken towards the routine contractual implementation of CALS in all new weapon system acquisitions and that on-going programs be reviewed for retrofit opportunities.

CALS is changing the way DoD does business by integrating contractor data systems and processes, providing specified government access to contractor databases and implementing digital interchange of technical information using international and national standards.

CALS: Objectives

The objectives of the CALS program are to improve the quality of weapon systems and their supporting technical data. Achieving these objectives will lead to increased operational readiness and industrial competitiveness. Some examples include:

1. *Improved industry responsiveness* will result from the development of integrated data, automation of plant facilities, and industrial networking.

2. *Shortened weapon system design, development, production and resupply time* will be possible through the creation of a shared data environment designed to generate and transfer data to appropriate functions.

3. *Reduced "out of service" times for repair and overhaul* will increase combat capability. This will be obtained from

integrated planning, automated tool design and setup, and more rapid parts support.

4. *The labor intensive development and duplicate data* used for separate processes in design, manufacturing, and support *will be eliminated.*

5. *The use of paper will be dramatically reduced* and replaced by accurate, timely, and cost effective digital technical information for acquisition, logistics, and field interoperability.

6. *Fewer errors in weapon system design and manufacturing* will result through integration of key databases which can support these functions in a near real time environment. Producibility, reliability, and maintainability considerations will be integrated with computer-aided engineering and design tools.

7. *Data consistency* will be significantly enhanced as databases are linked together.

CALS: Strategy

Weapon system programs provide the key mechanism to transition to a digital environment—taking advantage of the computer-aided design and manufacturing, and support information created in Industry. The Military Services have identified candidate weapon systems and are also evaluating CALS implementation opportunities to improve productivity and quality on existing weapon systems.

Five areas have been identified as being critical to the implementation of CALS. These are:

1. **Standards:** CALS will leverage existing international and national standards.

2. **Technology Development and Demonstration:** Development and demonstration of technologies that can support the integration, management and secure dissemination of large volumes of digitized data.

3. **Acquisition:** Includes implementation policy, program management guidance, and contracting language for weapon system acquisitions.

4. **DoD Infrastructure Modernization:** Addresses fundamental changes in the way DoD receives and uses technical data.

5. **Training and Outreach:** Addresses the culture change needed to effectively implement CALS throughout the defense establishment.

GLOSSARY

CALS (See Computer Acquisition and Logistic Support)

CFM/pro™ is the trade name of software developed to help draft four-fields process maps (see Four-fields mapping) and to manage data and document resources associated with a particular cross-function process. It is the first example of a new generation of computer-based tools necessary to manage horizontal cross functions.

Collaboratory is an electronically supported knowledge team operating in four possible situations: people working at the same time in the same location; the same people working at the same time in different locations; people working in different locations at different times, or people working different times in the same location. Electronic technology plays a central role in making information available to groups in each of these four collaboratory situations. It creates the means for virtual proximity to take place.

Computer Acquisition and Logistic Support *(CALS)*, established by the Department of Defense (DoD) in 1985, is a DoD/Industry strategy for the transition to automated interchange of technical data, and to process improvements enabled by automation and integration.

Concurrent Engineering is a systematic approach to the integrated, concurrent design of products and their related processes, including manufacture and support. This approach is intended to cause the developers, from the outset, to consider all aspects of the product life cycle from conception through disposal, including quality, cost, schedule, and user requirements. (Definition from IDA Report R-338, 1988)

Concurrency is the parallel implementation of related activities. Concurrency works only if there is a disciplined method of linking those activities to ensure information flow and control of the outcome.

Control Panel describes an image on a terminal screen in which symbols are used to describe a total process. Much like a road or highway map consisting of symbols, a control panel can be used to describe a complicated process. New computer software technologies make it possible for the symbols to be "dynamic" in that a mouse pointed and clicked on a symbol can "open" it and lead to new layers of information or detail. A computer-based control panel is a natural supporting tool for cross-function process management.

Cross function   (See Functions)

Cross-Function Management is the body of methods, tools, and techniques necessary for a company-wide team to manage a cross-function process such as quality assurance, cost control, product development, personnel training, or information integration.

Four-fields mapping is the name given to the integration of four process elements: team membership, phasing and milestones, task flow and control, and guidelines and standards.

Four-fields template is a visual description of the four process elements being mapped. It is usually presented on a single sheet of paper (8x10 or 8x14). More detailed descriptions of a process element, such as a complex task, are depicted in secondary or tertiary templates.

Functions: vertical and cross

A *vertical function* is generally associated with a chimneylike or top-down organizational structure such as Engineering, Marketing, Sales, or Finance. Its purpose is to produce "results" or output that is measurable in cost or revenue terms.

A *cross function* is generally associated with horizontal process activities that focus on how things are done rather than on results. A cross function focuses on process issues of companywide importance to an enterprise. These include such things as quality assurance, cost control, product development, personnel training, or information integration.

Groupware describes electronic tools (hardware, software, and communication) used to support the activities of groups of individuals located in single or multiple sites or working simultaneously or at different times on shared tasks.

Holistic management takes the "whole" system into account rather than single parts independent of the whole. Conventional management practices are not holistic because they allow compartmentalized or specialized departments to function at arm's length. This leads to what is commonly called "throw it over the wall" sequential management.

House of Quality (See Quality Tables)

Knowledge team describes a group that collectively represents know-how in a given area. Cross-function knowledge teams are companywide groups that together represent knowledge about a process such as cost control or quality assurance. This distinguishes them from individual departments or people who are "owners" of a given subject.

Learning organizations learn from prior experience. To do this they must develop methods for recording past experiences and making that knowledge available. Many of the tools and techniques associated with quality management are designed to institutionalize learning through "continuous improvement."

Marketing concept: "There is only one valid definition of business purpose: to create a satisfied customer. It is the customer who determines what the business is. Because it is its purpose to create a customer, any business has two and only these two basic functions: marketing and innovation.

"Actually marketing is so basic that it is not just enough to have a strong sales force and to entrust marketing to it. Marketing is not only much broader than selling, it is not a specialized activity at all. It is the whole business seeing the point of view of its final result, that is, from the customer's point of view." Peter F. Drucker [1954].

Policy deployment also known as Policy Function Deployment, is a top-down implementation of policy and goal directives. It is different from Management by Objective (MBO) in that it is not a negotiated process between executive and subordinate. Policy Deployment leaves it to subordinates to determine the best way in which they will achieve a corporate directive. This process is cascaded down through departments and sections and back up until there is deployment of the policy companywide. The goal is policy optimization.

Process is used to describe responsibilities for how things are done. There is no traditional structure in place in U.S. firms to oversee or reward process management. Process management has generally been delegated to staff or to administrative chimney. Cross functions are a breakthrough in defining responsibilities, structures, and methods for managing process companywide so as to optimize company performance.

Quality is the process of meeting customer-specified needs. Tools and techniques associated with quality management (the seven tools and seven new tools) are designed to empower employees in detecting errors, determining the causes, and correcting them wherever they exist in a system. Statistical process control is the most widely known technique for quality management.

Quality Tables (QT) sometimes described as the House of Quality, are matrices that array customer needs against solutions to those needs in a comprehensive format. They were first invented in Japan during the late 1960s and first applied in that country's shipbuilding industry a decade later. They were introduced to the United States by Don Clausing of MIT in 1984.

Quality Function Deployment (QFD) describes the overall process of applying various hierarchical levels of Quality Tables to a total process. The "Quality Function" refers to the companywide "cross function" focused on quality. It is a powerful method for meeting and deploying customer requirements laterally across departmental chimneys.

Results is a term used in this book to describe the principle focus of conventional management methods and techniques. A results-focused management system is driven by quantifiable measures such as time and cost. A results-based management system is not given to process management since the latter is viewed as inhibiting speedy achievement of results.

Scientific management is the name attached to a philosophy and practice of management originally espoused by Frederick Winslow Taylor late in the nineteenth century. His ideas embellished and altered by others eventually grew into a mainstream practice. One of the principal characteristics of scientific management was the "scientific" analysis of work tasks such that the best methods could be standardized and imposed on workers by managers. It eventually led to adversarial relationships between labor and management and to a fragmentation of work effort into highly specialized compartments. By the 1960s the first signs of the aging of these techniques came with the rapid evolution of a new set of quality management practices invented in the United States but widely applied in Japan.

Seamless management is a term used to explain a process in which there are few artificial hurdles to the flow of information within companies. These hurdles can be administrative, organizational, or even technological when equipment (for example, computer equipment) is pur-

GLOSSARY

chased that is not compatible with other equipment. Enterprise integration is synonymous with "seamless management."

Serialized (sequential) management is characterized by specialized activities that are completed one step at a time. This contrasts with activities that run parallel or concurrently. Serialized processes tend to take longer to complete and often require considerable rework since the product handed off from one task to the next does not always meet the needs of the "next person in line."

Stovepipes, or chimneys are names used to describe hierarchical organizational structures that are top-down in the flow of authority and that have evolved into insular entities with their own reward systems, languages, information resources, and administrative habits. This insularity and top-down flow of authority make fluid – or seamless – information flow across these chimneys difficult and inefficient.

Statistical Process Control (SPC) is the application of statistical sampling to any volume-based activity. The sampling allows a worker to monitor whether certain performance boundaries, such as tolerances, are under control, going out of control, or are out of control. The power of SPC is in allowing a worker to anticipate whether a process is gradually going out of control and if it is, to correct it before it does. This is a far less costly approach than waiting for a process to crash and then correcting it.

Systems are closed or open. A closed system is one in which an identifiable number of variables interact without any external interference. An open system is one in which a group of variables is influenced by external forces. A corporate "system" is not only highly complex but also "open." Numerous attempts have been made by systems analysts to quantify all the variables that constitute a system so that their behavior can be analyzed and anticipated. This has generally fallen short by failing to account for subjective variables such as human thought, emotions, and subjectivity, and by not being able to identify all the externalities that will affect a complex system.

Taylorism (see Scientific management)

Total Quality Control (TQC) is a body of tools and techniques necessary to monitor and control a process. Individuals such as W. Edwards Deming, Joseph Juran, Kaoru Ishikawa, and Genichi Taguchi are major figures in the development of TQC practices.

Total Quality Management (TQM) is TQC extended companywide. It includes methods and techniques necessary to manage process horizontally across company chimneys. In this book TQM is explained as

THE SEAMLESS ENTERPRISE

the marriage of Deming and Drucker philosophies and techniques. Cross-function management is a central operational feature of TQM.

Virtual meetings, laboratories, or groups are created by an electronic "intermediary" that allows people to meet without actually being in the same place and that allows an actual lab test to be simulated electronically without the person doing the test having to actually be in a laboratory.

SUGGESTED READING

Akao, Yoji, Ed., *Quality Function Deployment: Integrating Customer Requirements Into Product Design*, Cambridge, MA: Productivity, 1990.

Cusumano, Michael A., *Japan's Software Factories: A Challenge to U.S. Management*, New York, Oxford University Press, 1991: [Author's note: Superb insights into what makes Japanese management tick.]

Cusumano, Michael A., *The Japanese Automobile Industry*, Harvard University Press, 1985. [Author's note: Superb insights.]

Drucker, Peter F., *Management: Tasks-Responsibilities-Practices*, New York: Harper & Row, 1972.

Hanna, David P., *Designing Organizations for High Performance*, Reading, MA: Addison Wesley, 1988.

Imai, Masaaki , Kaizen, *The Key to Japan's Competitive Success*, New York: McGraw Hill, 1986.

Johnson, H. Thomas, and Robert S. Kaplan, *Relevance Lost: The Rise and Fall of Management Accounting*, Boston: Harvard Business School Press, 1987.

SUGGESTED READING

Mizuno, Shigeru, Ed., *Management for Quality Improvement: The 7 New QC Tools*, Cambridge, MA, Productivity, 1988.

Noble, David F., *Forces of Production*, New York: Knopf, 1984. [Author's note: This is an excellent book for understanding what went wrong with manufacturing automation in the United States.]

Pugh, D. S., Ed., *Organizational Theory*, New York: Viking Penguin, 1984.

Senge, Peter M., *The Fifth Discipline*, New York: Doubleday/Currency, 1990.

Stahl, Michael J., and Gregory M. Bounds, *Competing Globally Through Customer Value*, Westport, CT: Quorum Books, 1991. [Author's note: This book puts the University of Tennessee on the map for its broad faculty base in quality management.]

Strassman, Paul A., *The Information Payoff*, New York: The Free Press, 1985.

Taylor, Frederick Winslow, *Scientific Management*, New York: Harper & Brothers, 1947. [Author's note: This book is out of print but worth getting from a library, for "old time's sake," as a collection of Taylor's thoughts and practices.]

Zuboff, Shoshana, *In the Age of the Smart Machine*, New York: Basic Books, 1988.

INDEX